Crystallization-Study
of
1 Corinthians

Volume Two

Witness Lee

The Holy Word for Morning Revival

Living Stream Ministry
Anaheim, California

First Edition, February 2003.

ISBN 0-7363-2074-1
ISBN 0-7363-2072-5 (two-volume set)

Published by

Living Stream Ministry
2431 W. La Palma Ave., Anaheim, CA 92801 U.S.A.
P. O. Box 2121, Anaheim, CA 92814 U.S.A.

Printed in the United States of America

03 04 05 06 07 08 09 / 10 9 8 7 6 5 4 3 2 1

Contents

Preface

1. This book is intended as an aid to believers in developing a daily time of morning revival with the Lord in His word. At the same time, it provides a review of the 2002 Winter Training on the "Crystallization-study of 1 Corinthians." Through intimate contact with the Lord in His word, the believers can be constituted with life and truth and thereby equipped to prophesy in the meetings of the church unto the building up of the Body of Christ.

2. The content of this book is taken primarily from the *Crystallization-study Outlines,* the text and footnotes of the Recovery Version of the Bible, selections from the writings of Watchman Nee and Witness Lee, and *Hymns,* all of which are published by Living Stream Ministry.

3. The book is divided into weeks. One training message is covered per week. Each week first presents the message outline, followed by six daily portions, a hymn, and then some space for writing. The message outline has been divided into days, corresponding to the six daily portions. Each daily portion covers certain points and begins with a section entitled "Morning Nourishment." This section contains selected verses and a short reading that can provide rich spiritual nourishment through intimate fellowship with the Lord. The "Morning Nourishment" is followed by a section entitled "Today's Reading," a longer portion of ministry related to the day's main points. Each day's portion concludes with a short list of references for further reading and some space for the saints to make notes concerning their spiritual inspiration, enlightenment, and enjoyment to serve as a reminder of what they have received of the Lord that day.

4. The space provided at the end of each week is for composing a short prophecy. This prophecy can be composed by considering all of our daily notes, the "harvest" of our inspirations during the week, and preparing a main point with some sub-points to be spoken in the church meetings for the organic building up of the Body of Christ.

5. The *Crystallization-study Outlines* were compiled by Living Stream Ministry from the writings of Watchman Nee and Witness Lee. The outlines, footnotes, and references in the Recovery Version of the Bible were written by Witness Lee. All of the other references cited in this publication are from the ministry of Watchman Nee and Witness Lee.

2002 Winter Training

CRYSTALLIZATION-STUDY
OF 1 CORINTHIANS

Banners:

God has called us into the fellowship of His Son
that we may partake of Christ and enjoy Him
as our unique center and as our God-given portion.

The enjoyment of the crucified Christ
as the life-giving Spirit in our spirit
solves all the problems in the church
and issues in the growth in life
for the building up of the church.

The essence of the New Testament is the two spirits—
the divine Spirit and the human spirit—
mingled together as one spirit.

Love is the most excellent way
and prophesying is the excelling gift
for the building up of the church.

The Lord's Table and the Lord's Supper

Scripture Reading: 1 Cor. 10:14-22; 11:17-34

Day 1

I. **The record regarding spiritual eating in the Bible is a strong indication that God intends to dispense Himself into us by the way of eating (Gen. 2:9, 16-17; Exo. 12:1-11; 16:14-15; Deut. 8:7-10; Rev. 2:7, 17; 3:20; 22:14):**

A. To eat is to contact things outside of us and to receive them into us, with the result that they eventually become our constitution (Gen. 2:16-17).

Day 2

B. Food is anything we take into us for our satisfaction; whatever we desire, hunger, and thirst after is the diet according to which our being has been constituted (Job 23:12b; Jer. 15:16; Num. 11:4-6).

C. What a person eats gets into him and causes him to become an expression of that thing; this is based on the principle that eating is a fellowship, a participation (1 Cor. 10:16, 21).

D. Eating is the way to experience God's dispensing and to be mingled with Him for His expression (Gen. 1:26; 2:9).

E. We are what we eat; therefore, if we eat God as our food, we will be one with God and even become God in life and in nature but not in the Godhead (John 6:32-33, 35, 41, 48, 50-51).

F. We live according to that with which we are occupied and saturated; if we eat Christ and are saturated with Him as the life-giving Spirit, we shall live Christ (v. 57; Phil. 1:21a).

G. The entire Christian life should be a feast, an enjoyment of Christ as our banquet (1 Cor. 5:7-8; 10:16-17):

1. We should all eat the same spiritual food, not eating anything other than the Lord or enjoying anything in place of the Lord (vv. 3-4).

2. Eating is related to enjoyment; if our enjoyment is something other than Christ, then
in the sight of God that enjoyment is idolatry (vv. 7, 14, 22).

Day 3   II. **The emphasis of the Lord's table is the fellowship of His blood and body, the participa-
tion in the Lord, the enjoyment of the Lord
in mutuality, in fellowship (vv. 16-17, 21):**
A. The Lord has given Himself to us that we may
partake of Him and enjoy Him by eating and
drinking Him:
1. The One who presents His body and blood
to us is Christ as the all-inclusive Spirit
(15:45b; 2 Cor. 3:17).
2. This wonderful Christ is everything to us
for our enjoyment; all that He is, is for our
participation and enjoyment.
B. "The cup of blessing which we bless, is it not
the fellowship of the blood of Christ? The
bread which we break, is it not the fellowship
of the body of Christ?" (1 Cor. 10:16):
1. *Fellowship* here refers to the believers'
communion in the joint participation in the
blood and body of Christ.
2. The fellowship makes us, the participants in
the Lord's blood and body, not only one with
one another but also one with the Lord; we
make ourselves identified with the Lord in
the fellowship of His blood and body.
3. In 1:9 the fellowship is the fellowship of the
Son of God; in 10:16 the fellowship is the
fellowship of His blood and body, indicating
that He has been processed for our enjoyment.
C. "Seeing that there is one bread, we who are
many are one Body, for we all partake of the
one bread" (v. 17):
1. We are all one Body because we all partake
of the one bread; our joint partaking of the
one bread makes us all one.

2. Our partaking of Christ makes us all His one Body; the very Christ of whom we all partake constitutes us His one Body.

Day 4

D. The table with the body and blood of Christ is the reality of Christ as the good land; whenever we come to the Lord's table to enjoy Him as the all-inclusive One, in our experience we are in the good land enjoying the riches of the land.

E. Our participation in the Lord's table must be in the unique fellowship of His unique Body, without any division either in practice or in spirit.

Day 5

III. **The emphasis of the Lord's supper is the remembrance of the Lord (11:24-25):**

A. At the Lord's table we receive His body and blood for our enjoyment; at the Lord's supper we give Him our remembrance for His enjoyment.

B. Regarding the Lord's table and the Lord's supper, there is mutuality; the Lord's table is for our enjoyment, and the Lord's supper is for His enjoyment.

C. The word *unto* in verses 24 and 25 implies a result—a continual remembrance of the Lord for His satisfaction.

Day 6

D. The real remembrance of the Lord is to eat the bread and drink the cup (vv. 24-25):

1. The bread is of life, and the cup is of blessing (John 6:35; 1 Cor. 10:16).

2. To eat the bread and drink the cup is to take in the redeeming Lord as our portion, our life and blessing; this is to remember Him in a genuine way.

E. "As often as you eat this bread and drink the cup, you declare the Lord's death until He comes" (11:26):

1. To take the Lord's supper is not to remember the Lord's death but to declare and display it.

2. We should take the Lord's supper unto the remembrance of Him by declaring His redeeming death until He comes back to set up God's kingdom (Matt. 26:29).

3. When we eat the Lord's supper with a view to a continual remembrance of Him in His first and second comings, that supper becomes a satisfaction to Him in relation to the kingdom, God's administration.

F. In taking the Lord's supper we must discern the Body to determine whether the bread on the table represents the unique mystical Body of Christ (1 Cor. 11:29).

G. Eating the Lord's supper should remind us to live a life in the church to bring in the kingdom for the satisfaction of the Lord Jesus (v. 26; Matt. 26:29).

Morning Nourishment

Gen. And out of the ground Jehovah God caused to
2:9 grow every tree that is pleasant to the sight and
good for food, as well as the tree of life in the
middle of the garden and the tree of the knowledge of good and evil.

Rev. ...To him who overcomes, to him I will give to eat
2:7 of the tree of life, which is in the Paradise of God.

22:14 Blessed are those who wash their robes that they
may have right to the tree of life and may enter
by the gates into the city.

Eating the bread of the Lord's table indicates that the Lord
comes into us as our life supply and then actually becomes us.
If we consider the matter of eating, we shall realize that the
food we eat eventually becomes us....Not only is there an
organic union between us and the food we eat, digest, and
assimilate; we are mingled with the food we assimilate into us.

In a similar way, when we take in the Triune God as our
food, we are truly mingled with Him. In order for the food we
eat to become our life, it must be mingled with us. The principle
is the same with taking in the Triune God as our food. (*Life-
study of Mark,* pp. 384-385)

Today's Reading

According to Genesis 1, God created man in His image with
the intention of dispensing Himself into man....God's way to
dispense Himself into man is through man's eating of Him as
the tree of life [2:9]. The eating of the tree of life implies two
things: first, that life is the means for God to dispense Himself
into us; second, that eating is the way God is dispensed into us.
If we would have God's dispensing, we need both life as the
means and eating as the way.

The matter of eating is found throughout the Bible, from the
beginning in Genesis to the end in Revelation. We have the tree
of life in Genesis 2, and we have the tree of life again in Revelation 22. Between Genesis 2 and Revelation 22 there is a line

related to eating. At the time of the Passover the children of Israel ate the meat of the lamb in order to receive the life supply (Exo. 12:3-5, 8-9). Then in the wilderness they were sustained by manna (Exo. 16:14-15). Manna was their food, and by eating manna they received the supply of life. Eventually, the children of Israel entered into the good land, and there they enjoyed the rich produce of the land (Josh. 5:12). Three times a year the people came together to eat the produce of the good land before God and with God. In their feasts they were eating, and God was eating as well.

In the New Testament, the Lord Jesus in John 6 says that He is the bread of life and that we need to eat Him (vv. 35, 51, 56-57). If we eat Him as the bread of life, we shall live by Him. Paul speaks also about eating the spiritual food in his Epistles. In 1 Corinthians 10:3 he says, "All ate the same spiritual food." In Revelation 2:7 and 22:14 the Lord speaks about eating the tree of life.

The record regarding the spiritual eating in the Bible is a strong indication and implication that God intends to dispense Himself into our being by means of life and by the way of eating. God is life to us, and the way we take Him as life is to eat Him.

During the past centuries there have been those who received God's dispensing, the saints who contacted God all the time. Even though they may not have known the word *dispensing* or had the adequate knowledge about eating God, they took God into them as their food. For the most part, they ate God by eating the Word. The Word conveys God as its content. Apart from God as the content of the Word, the Word is empty. Hence, to eat the words of the Bible is actually to eat God conveyed in the Word. (*The Conclusion of the New Testament*, pp. 124-125)

Further Reading: Life-study of Mark, msg. 44; The Conclusion of the New Testament, msgs. 12, 42; Eating the Lord, chs. 1-4; Life-study of 1 John, msgs. 18-19; The Divine Dispensing for the Divine Economy, ch. 1

Enlightenment and inspiration: _____

_____

_____

_____

Morning Nourishment

1 Cor. And all ate the same spiritual food, and all drank the
10:3-4 same spiritual drink; for they drank of a spiritual
rock which followed *them*, and the rock was Christ.
14 Therefore, my beloved, flee from idolatry.
Num. But now our appetite has gone; there is nothing at
11:6 all but this manna to look at.

We have seen that Paul likens our enjoyment of the Lord's
table to the enjoyment of those Israelites who ate the sacrifices
and who thus were fellowshippers of the altar (1 Cor. 10:18).
We need to be impressed with the fact that eating is related to
enjoyment. If our enjoyment is of something other than Christ,
then in the sight of God that enjoyment is idolatry. We need to
simplify and purify our enjoyment so that we enjoy only the
Lord Himself. (*Life-study of 1 Corinthians*, p. 453)

Today's Reading

In the wilderness God gave the children of Israel nothing except
manna to eat. According to Numbers 11:6, the people complained,
"But now our appetite has gone; there is nothing at all but this
manna to look at." How marvelous it was that God gave the people
nothing except manna! This indicates that He gave them nothing except Christ. I thank the Lord that a good number of the
church people do not have an appetite for anything other than
Christ. Day by day, the hunger of many in the churches is for
Christ and Christ alone. We thirst for Him and desire to contact
Him, to read the Word, to call on His name, and to read the
printed messages. Truly the Lord has changed our diet.

I can testify that I live on the Lord Jesus Christ, not on
anything else. Frequently, I read a newspaper. But whenever
a newspaper becomes part of my diet, I immediately repent,
confess, and ask the Lord to forgive me for turning to something
other than Him to satisfy my desire. Whenever we hunger and
thirst for something other than Christ, we are wrong.

It is important to understand this message in a proper way.
My burden is not to issue a charge to the saints about the love

of the world. It is to point out the need for a change in our diet. May the Lord take away the desire and hunger for anything other than Christ! We need clothing and a proper dwelling place. However, our appetite, our desire, should not be for these things. Our appetite should be for Christ. We should not try to find satisfaction in clothing or in a better house. God has changed our diet from the things of Egypt to Christ alone.

This does not mean that we are to live as if we were monks or nuns. We are not to be like the Amish, who are allowed to wear only certain colors. The sisters need to dress in a suitable way, but they should not have an appetite for fashion or style. Instead, their appetite should be for Christ. We all need to say, "Lord Jesus, I love You. I want to breathe You, drink You, and eat You. Lord, I long to feast on You." Our hunger, thirst, desire, and appetite should be for Christ as the heavenly manna.

Over a period of forty years, God gave the children of Israel nothing to eat except manna....From John 6 we...know that this heavenly manna is a type of Christ. Christ came from God to be our diet. We need to eat Him, drink Him, and breathe Him. We need a change in our inward constitution, not merely a change in our outward behavior. If we would have such an inward change, we need to have a change of food supply, for the food we eat is the source of our constitution. Dietitians tell us that we are what we eat. The food we eat enters into us organically and becomes our constitution. As God's people today, we need to be reconstituted with Christ as our very element. In this way, we shall become Christ as far as our constitution is concerned....This change of constitution through a change of diet is altogether different from the methods of self-improvement practiced in religion. (*Life-study of Exodus,* pp. 406-407)

Further Reading: Life-study of 1 Corinthians, msgs. 50-51; *Life-study of Exodus,* msg. 34; *Life-study of Leviticus,* msg. 12; *The Experience and Growth in Life,* msgs. 1-2; *Enjoying the Riches of Christ for the Building Up of the Church as the Body of Christ,* ch. 5

Enlightenment and inspiration: _____

_____
_____
_____

Morning Nourishment

1 Cor. **The cup of blessing which we bless, is it not the**
10:16-17 **fellowship of the blood of Christ? The bread which**
we break, is it not the fellowship of the body of Christ?
Seeing that there is one bread, we who are many
are one Body; for we all partake of the one bread.
1:9 **God is faithful, through whom you were called into**
the fellowship of His Son, Jesus Christ our Lord.

The Greek word rendered *fellowship* also means "joint participation." *Fellowship* here refers to the believer's communion
in the joint participation in the blood and body of Christ. This
makes us, the participants of the Lord's blood and body, not
only one with one another, but also one with the Lord. We, the
participants, make ourselves identified with the Lord in the
fellowship of His blood and body. The apostle's thought here is
to illustrate how eating and drinking make the eaters and
drinkers one with what they eat and drink. The Corinthians
should realize that their abusive eating of idol sacrifices actually makes them one with the demons behind the sacrifices.

In 1 Corinthians 10:17 Paul speaks a strong word concerning
the one bread and the one Body....We are all one bread, one Body,
because we all partake of the one bread. Our joint partaking of
the one bread makes us all one. This indicates that our partaking
of Christ makes us all His one Body. The very Christ of whom we
all partake constitutes us into His one Body. Partaking of the
one bread, that is, eating of it (vv. 28-30), identifies us with it.
This means that our partaking of Christ, our enjoyment of
Christ, identifies us with Him, making us one with Him.

Christ is the Lord and He is also the table....The table is
typified by the good land, which was a table to the children of
Israel. When they dwelt in the good land, they feasted on the
table, enjoying all the rich produce of the land. The various
aspects of the produce of the land are types of the riches of
Christ. Furthermore, Christ Himself is to us the good land as
the table. If we see this picture clearly, we shall know how to
enjoy the Lord as the good land with all the riches. (*Life-study
of 1 Corinthians,* pp. 438-439, 453)

Today's Reading

God has called us into the fellowship of His Son, Jesus Christ our Lord....Fellowship involves participation. Now I wish to say that fellowship includes enjoyment....To enter into the fellowship of the Son is to come into the enjoyment of Him [1 Cor. 1:9]. In 1:9 the fellowship is the fellowship of a person....In 10:16 the fellowship is of that person's blood and body. When the Lord Jesus ate with His disciples and established the table, He "took bread and blessed it, and He broke it and gave it to the disciples, and said, Take, eat; this is My body" (Matt. 26:26). Then taking the cup and giving thanks, "He gave it to them, saying, Drink of it, all of you" (v. 27). Today the Lord invites us to His table and says of the bread and the cup, "This is My body; take and eat....This is My blood; take and drink."...By speaking in this way concerning His body and blood, the Lord is presenting Himself to us for our enjoyment. He gives Himself to us as our food supply so that we may enjoy Him. Oh, may the Lord open our eyes!...He has given us Himself so that we may partake of Him and enjoy Him by eating and drinking Him.

As the all-inclusive One who presents Himself to us for our enjoyment, Christ is the embodiment of the Triune God, the Father, the Son, and the Spirit. He is the very God incarnate, the One who lived on earth as a man for thirty-three and a half years, who died on the cross to terminate the old creation, who was resurrected physically and spiritually, and who became through resurrection the life-giving Spirit. Today the One who presents His body and blood to us is Christ as the life-giving Spirit. This wonderful Christ is everything to us for our enjoyment. All that He is, is for our participation and enjoyment. (*Life-study of 1 Corinthians,* pp. 447-448)

Further Reading: Life-study of 1 Corinthians, msgs. 49-51; *Basic Lessons on Service,* lsns. 2-3

Enlightenment and inspiration: _____
_____
_____
_____

Morning Nourishment

1 Cor.
10:21   You cannot drink the Lord's cup and the demons' cup; you cannot partake of the Lord's table and of the demons' table.

Deut.
8:7   For Jehovah your God is bringing you to a good land, a land of waterbrooks, of springs and of fountains, flowing forth in valleys and in mountains.

9-10   A land in which you will eat bread without scarcity; you will not lack anything in it; a land whose stones are iron, and from whose mountains you can mine copper. And you shall eat and be satisfied, and you shall bless Jehovah your God for the good land which He has given you.

The proper way to deal with eating is to feast on the Lord. Do not eat anything other than the Lord, and do not enjoy anything in place of Him. We should not have any enjoyment other than Christ. Christ is our table, our feast, our land. As the good land, Christ is a rich feast for our enjoyment. When we feast on Him, we live Him. Then we are able to defeat the enemies, establish the kingdom of God, and build up His temple. This is God's goal and the fulfillment of His eternal purpose. (*Life-study of 1 Corinthians,* pp. 451-452)

Today's Reading

Whenever we come to the Lord's table to enjoy Christ as the all-inclusive One, in our experience we are in the good land enjoying the riches of the land. This means that the good land has become a table, a feast, for our enjoyment. At this table, this feast, we are satisfied, and God is satisfied also....Praise the Lord that when we come to the table, we enter into the good land!

Our understanding of the Lord's table has been limited by the influence of our religious background and also by our natural concepts....[This is not] merely to attend a meeting centered around a table with a loaf and a cup. We may not have any realization in our spirit that by coming to the table and enjoying it, we are enjoying Christ as the all-inclusive land.

Do you know how the children of Israel established the kingdom of God on earth and how they built the temple of God? They did this through the enjoyment of the riches of the good land. Because the children of Israel enjoyed these riches, they could defeat their enemies. The riches of the land not only enabled the people to live; they also equipped them to fight and bring in the kingdom of God. Furthermore, the riches of the land supplied them with what they needed to build God's temple. Therefore, both the kingdom of God and the temple come into being through the enjoyment of the riches of the good land. The riches of the land were the source of the living of the children of Israel. These riches were also the supply for them to defeat the enemy, establish the kingdom of God, and build the temple of God. One day the glory of God descended and filled this temple. That was the consummate result of the enjoyment of the riches of the good land.

The experience of the children of Israel in the good land typifies our enjoyment of Christ today. Christ is our good land, and the various aspects of the riches of Christ are typified by the produce of the land. If we enjoy the rich supply of Christ, we shall be able to live Christ. We shall also be empowered to defeat the enemies. The enemies are always defeated when we enjoy Christ. Furthermore, through the enjoyment of the riches of Christ, the kingdom of God is established in the church, and the temple is built for God's dwelling place. All these matters— living the Christian life, defeating the enemies, establishing the kingdom of God, and building the house of God—issue out from the enjoyment of the riches of Christ.

Now we must see that these riches are displayed on the Lord's table. Therefore, the table is a feast for our enjoyment. Many of us have been attending the Lord's table for years, but we have never had this understanding of the table. It is crucial for us to understand that to come to the table is to enjoy Christ as the good land. (*Life-study of 1 Corinthians,* pp. 448-449)

Further Reading: Life-study of 1 Corinthians, msg. 50

Enlightenment and inspiration: _____

_____

_____

_____

Morning Nourishment

1 Cor. For I received from the Lord that which also I
11:23-26 delivered to you, that the Lord Jesus in the night
in which He was betrayed took bread, and having
given thanks, He broke it and said, This is My
body, which is *given* for you; this do unto the
remembrance of Me. Similarly also the cup after
they had dined, saying, This cup is the new covenant *established* in My blood; this do, as often as
you drink *it,* unto the remembrance of Me. For as
often as you eat this bread and drink the cup, you
declare the Lord's death until He comes.

What Paul received from the Lord he delivered to the
Corinthian believers [1 Cor. 11:23-26]....The breaking of the
bread is that we may eat it (Matt. 26:26). To take the Lord's
supper is for the remembrance of the Lord Himself.

The bread is of life (John 6:35), and the cup is of blessing
(1 Cor. 10:16). This cup is the new covenant, made up of all the
rich blessings of the New Testament, including God Himself. It
was enacted by the Lord's blood, which He shed on the cross for
our redemption (Matt. 26:28).

The real remembrance of the Lord is to eat the bread and
drink the cup (1 Cor. 11:26), that is, to participate in, to enjoy, the
Lord who has given Himself to us through His redeeming death.
To eat the bread and drink the cup is to take in the redeeming
Lord as our portion, as our life and blessing. This is to remember
Him in a genuine way. (*Life-study of 1 Corinthians,* pp. 489-490)

Today's Reading

When we come to the Lord's table, our concern is neither
redemption nor the divine administration; our concern is for
enjoyment. We all come to the Lord's table to enjoy the Lord in
fellowship. We probably do not have any thought of God's
administration. The Lord's supper, however, is related to the
Lord's enjoyment and satisfaction. We should not only care for our
enjoyment at the table, but also care for the Lord's enjoyment

at the supper....We may care for our satisfaction, but not care for the Lord's satisfaction. Therefore, we need more light from the Lord concerning the Lord's supper. This will cause our meetings around His table to be improved. We shall praise the Lord that the supper is for His remembrance, enjoyment, and satisfaction. We shall realize that we are not only for our satisfaction, but even the more for God to be satisfied by Him.

If we want the Lord Jesus to be satisfied at the Lord's supper, we should not only remember Him, but also care for God's administration carried out by Him. Today what satisfies the Lord the most is the divine administration....If we want to make Him happy and satisfy Him, we must be able to say, "Lord, while we are remembering You, we discern Your Body for God's administration carried out by You. As we remember You, we do not forget what You are doing in the heavens. You are seated in the heavens to carry out God's administration."

In chapter ten Paul does not say anything about participating in the Lord's table until He comes. But in 11:26 he says, "For as often as you eat this bread and drink the cup, you declare the Lord's death until He comes." The Lord's coming will bring in God's kingdom for His administration. His first coming was for our redemption, but His second coming will be for God's administration. When we take of the Lord's table, we care for our enjoyment. But when we take of the Lord's supper, we care for His remembrance and God's administration...for His enjoyment and satisfaction. Furthermore, His satisfaction is dependent on God's administration carried out by Him. Do you intend to give the Lord the best remembrance? If you do, then you must take care of the mystical Body, the means for Him to carry out God's administration on earth. We must remember Him in this way until He comes. We do this to carry out His administration until He comes back and brings His kingdom to earth. (*Life-study of 1 Corinthians,* pp. 481-483)

Further Reading: Life-study of 1 Corinthians, msgs. 54-56; *Elders' Training, Book 6: The Crucial Points of the Truth in Paul's Epistles,* ch. 3

Enlightenment and inspiration: _____
_____
_____
_____

Morning Nourishment

1 Cor. **For as often as you eat this bread and drink the**
11:26 **cup, you declare the Lord's death until He comes.**
   29 **For he who eats and drinks, eats and drinks judg-**
        ment to himself if he does not discern the body.
Matt. **But I say to you, I shall by no means drink of this**
26:29 **product of the vine from now on until that day when**
        I drink it new with you in the kingdom of My Father.

[A] crucial word used by Paul is *discern* [1 Cor. 11:29]....This
is the discerning both of the Lord's physical body and also of the
mystical Body for the carrying out of God's administration.
Proving ourselves is for the remembrance of the Lord; discerning the Body is mainly for the carrying out of God's administration. Whenever we come to the Lord's table, we should not just
enjoy the Lord; we should also remember Him by proving
ourselves. We must ask if we are living in a way that is worthy
for us to eat the Lord's supper. We should never take the Lord's
blood and body in a careless manner. Instead, we should realize
that the signs on the table signify the precious blood and body
of the Lord. Then we must ask ourselves if we live and behave
in a way that is worthy of our eating this supper. This is to
remember the Lord. At the same time we must discern whether
the bread on the table signifies the unique mystical Body of
Christ or if it signifies a division. If the bread signifies a certain
divisive group or denomination, we should not take it, for we
discern the Body. To discern the Body in this way is to recognize
that it is utterly distinct from anything divisive. We discern the
Body in such a way for the carrying out of God's administration.
(*Life-study of 1 Corinthians*, pp. 485-486)

Today's Reading

Now we must go on further to see why we need to eat the
Lord's supper....We should come to the Lord's supper with the
expectation that a certain result will issue forth. Our eating of
the Lord's supper must result in the remembrance of the Lord
in His two comings. We should remember Him in His first

coming to accomplish the all-inclusive redemption to produce the church, and also in His second coming to bring in the kingdom so that both God and we may have a way to carry on the recovery. Apart from the kingdom, there is no way for the Lord's recovery to be carried onward. Therefore, we eat the Lord's supper with a view to remembering Him in both His first coming and in His second coming.

To remember the Lord in this way actually is to satisfy Him. The Lord has come and has died on the cross to produce the church. He is very happy with what He has accomplished and what He has produced. Now He is in the heavens carrying on His heavenly ministry so that He may come back to earth with the kingdom of His Father.

Truly the church is Christ's satisfaction. Whenever we come to eat the Lord's supper, we declare His death. We announce to the whole universe that the Lord Jesus has come, that He has died on the cross to accomplish an all-inclusive redemption, and that His death has produced the church. Now we are the church, His Body, responding to His ministry in the heavens and cooperating with Him. To eat His supper on the first day of every week is to make such a declaration. As long as there is a people on earth responding to Christ in His heavenly ministry, there is a way for Him to bring God's kingdom to earth. This is what satisfies the Lord and makes Him happy.

The Lord's supper should serve as a reminder that we are living on the earth for the Lord's satisfaction. Yes, the supper is for us to eat, but it is not for our satisfaction. We eat the supper not for our satisfaction, but for the Lord's satisfaction. Eating the supper reminds us to have a life in the church to bring in the kingdom for the satisfaction of the Lord Jesus. Therefore, this supper is a satisfaction to the Lord in relation to the kingdom, the administration of God. (*Life-study of 1 Corinthians,* pp. 503-505)

Further Reading: Life-study of 1 Corinthians, msgs. 54-56;
The Lord's Table Meeting (Outlines), otls. 1-2, 5-6

Enlightenment and inspiration: _____

_____

_____

_____

Hymns, #221

1   Lord, we thank Thee for the table,
     With the bread and with the wine;
  At this table we enjoy Thee
    As the feast of love divine.
  We partake the bread, the emblem
     Of Thy body giv'n for us;
  And we share the wine, the symbol
    Of Thy blood Thou shedd'st for us.

      Lo, the holy table!
      With the sacred symbols;
      Its significance in figure
      Is unsearchable!

2   By the death of Thy redemption,
    That Thy life Thou may impart,
  E'en Thyself to us Thou gavest
    That we share in all Thou art.
  By the bread and wine partaking,
    We Thy death display and prove;
  Eating, drinking of Thyself, Lord,
    We remember Thee with love.

3   By this bread which signifieth
    Thy one body mystical,
  We commune with all Thy members
    In one bond identical.
  By this holy cup of blessing,
    Cup of wine which now we bless,
  Of Thy blood we have communion
    With all those who faith possess.

4   Thou art our eternal portion,
    Here we take a sweet foretaste;
  We are waiting for Thy kingdom,
    And Thy coming now we haste.
  At Thy coming, in Thy kingdom,
    With all saints that overcome,
  We anew will feast upon Thee
    And Thy loving Bride become.

Composition for prophecy with main point and sub-points: _____

_____

_____

_____

_____

_____

_____

_____

_____

_____

_____

_____

_____

_____

_____

_____

_____

_____

_____

_____

_____

_____

_____

_____

_____

_____

_____

_____

_____

_____

_____

_____

_____

_____

_____

_____

The Body of Christ—the Means of the Divine Administration

Scripture Reading: 1 Cor. 12:12-27

Day 1 I. **The apostle's dealing with head covering concerns the Head; his dealing with the Lord's supper (the Lord's table) concerns the Body (11:3, 17-34):**
A. Regarding the headship of Christ, which represents God and is represented by man, we must keep the divine governmental order ordained by God, without any disorder.
B. Regarding the Body of Christ, we must be properly regulated by the apostle's instruction, without any confusion or division.
C. The Head is Christ, and the Body is the church (v. 3; 1:2; 12:27); these two—Christ and the church—are the controlling and directing factors of the apostle's dealing with the confused and disorderly church:
1. In chapters one through ten Paul deals with the church's problems first by stressing Christ as God's center and our portion.
2. In chapters eleven through sixteen he emphasizes the church as God's goal and our concern.
3. Both Christ and the church are crucial to the carrying out of God's administration in His New Testament economy.

Day 2 & Day 3 II. **The unique mystical Body of Christ is the means for God to carry out His administration (Rom. 12:4-5; Eph. 1:22-23; 1 Cor. 12:12-13, 25, 27; 11:29):**
A. The mystical Body of Christ is thoroughly and absolutely related to God's administration; apart from the mystical Body of Christ, God has no means, no way, to carry out His administration.
B. God's eternal purpose is to have a group of saved

and regenerated people who have become one to
be an organic Body to carry out His administration (Eph. 3:10-11; 4:16; 1 Cor. 1:2; 12:12-13, 27).

C. The mystical Body of Christ, the church, is for
Christ's move on earth; the Head is now operating God's administration through the Body (11:3;
12:12).

D. Divisions damage the mystical Body of Christ
with respect to the carrying out of God's administration (1:2, 10-13; 12:25, 27):

1. Satan's subtle device is to cut the Body into
pieces.

2. For centuries God has not been able to
carry out His administration because the
unique means for this—the mystical Body of
Christ—has been cut into pieces through
division.

3. Because we realize that the carrying out of
the divine administration requires the
unique Body, the mystical Body, we hate division and are absolutely opposed to it (1:10;
12:25; Acts 20:30; Rom. 16:17-18; Titus 3:10).

4. In order that God's administration may be
carried out, we must care for the oneness of
the unique mystical Body of Christ (Eph. 4:3,
13; John 17:21-23); having such a concern will
preserve us in the Body and keep us from any
division.

E. We take care of God's administration by discerning the Body (1 Cor. 11:29):

1. To discern the Body is first to realize that
Christ has only one mystical Body.

2. If we have the proper understanding of the
Lord's supper, we shall not be divided by
anything; rather, we shall remain in the
unique mystical Body of Christ, the means
for Christ to carry out His heavenly ministry
for the accomplishment of the divine administration.

Day 4 **III. The Body of Christ is the corporate Christ (12:12-13):**

  A. In verse 12 *the Christ* refers not to the individual Christ but to the corporate Christ, the Body-Christ:

  1. The corporate Christ is composed of Christ Himself as the Head and the church as His Body with all the believers as His members.

  2. All the believers in Christ are organically united with Him (Rom. 12:4-5) and constituted with His life and element (Col. 3:4, 11) and have thus become His Body, an organism to express Him; hence, Christ is not only the Head but also the Body.

  3. The Bible considers Christ and the church as one mysterious Christ (Acts 9:4-5):

    a. Christ is the Head of this mysterious Christ, and the church is the Body of this mysterious Christ; the two have been joined to become the one mysterious Christ (Eph. 5:32).

    b. All the saved ones in all times and all space added together become the Body of this mysterious Christ.

  B. Because the reality of Christ is the Spirit, the way to be constituted with Christ to be His Body is to drink the Spirit (1 Cor. 12:13):

  1. The baptism into the one Body has positioned us all to drink one Spirit.

  2. By drinking of the Spirit we are constituted to be the Body.

Day 5 **IV. Blending is the most helpful thing in keeping the oneness of the Body (vv. 24-25):**

  A. The universal Body of Christ is a blending of all the local churches in the divine life (Col. 4:15-16; Rev. 1:4, 11; 2:7a).

  B. The goal of the universal blending is the reality of the Body of Christ.

C. Blending requires us to be crossed out and be by the Spirit to dispense Christ and do everything for the sake of His Body.

D. Blending means that we should always stop to fellowship with others; to have fellowship is to put away our private interests and join with others for a common purpose—the building up of the Body of Christ to consummate the New Jerusalem (1 John 1:3; Eph. 4:16; Rev. 21:2).

E. In the spiritual element all the churches should be blended together as one.

Day 6 V. **The one Body is the one church of God, manifested in many localities as many local churches (Eph. 1:22; 1 Cor. 10:32b; 1:2; 12:27; Rev. 1:4, 11):**

A. The local churches are many in existence but are still one Body universally in element (Eph. 4:4).

B. All the local churches are and should be one Body universally, doctrinally, and practically (1 Cor. 4:17; 7:17; 11:16; 14:33; 16:1).

Morning Nourishment

1 Cor. To the church of God which is in Corinth...with all
  1:2   those who call upon the name of our Lord Jesus
        Christ in every place, *who is* theirs and ours.
  11:3 But I want you to know that Christ is the head of
        every man, and the man is the head of the woman,
        and God is the head of Christ.
  12:27 Now you are the Body of Christ, and members
        individually.

The apostle's dealing with head covering is related to the
Head (1 Cor. 11:3); his dealing with the Lord's supper (the
Lord's table) is related to the Body. Regarding the headship of
Christ, representing God and represented by man, we must
keep the divine governmental order ordained by God without
any disorder. Regarding the Body of Christ, we must be properly regulated by the apostle's instruction without any confusion or division. The Head is Christ, and the Body is the church.
Christ and the church—these two—are the controlling and
directing factors of the apostle's dealings with the confused and
disorderly church. He deals with the church's problems first by
stressing Christ as God's center and our portion in chapters one
through ten. Following this, he emphasizes the church as God's
goal and our concern in chapters eleven through sixteen. In
chapters one through ten he begins with Christ as the antibiotic
to heal the diseases of the sick church. Then from chapter eleven
he goes on to the church and uses the matter of the church, the
Body, as an inoculation against the church's disorder. Both
Christ and the church are crucial to the carrying out of God's
administration in His New Testament economy. (*Life-study of
1 Corinthians,* p. 492)

Today's Reading

In 1 Corinthians eleven problems are dealt with by the
apostle....These eleven problems are in two categories. The first
group is composed of the six problems covered in chapters one
through ten.

These six problems all belong to the realm of human life....The factor needed for solving these problems concerning the proper daily Christian life is Christ. Christ is God's center and the One given to us as our unique portion. If we enjoy Christ according to the way He is revealed in the first ten chapters of this book, we shall have the necessary factor to solve these six problems.

The problems among the Corinthians, however, were related not only to human living, but even the more to God's administration....The first of the five problems related to God's administration is that of headship. Paul covers this in 11:2-16 when he deals with head covering. Head covering is related to the headship in God's universal, governmental administration.

The second problem in this group is that of the Lord's supper. The Lord's supper is not a thing in itself, for it concerns the Body. For God to administrate the universe He needs the Body. He needs a group of people formed organically into a Body. This Body is the means by which God carries out His administration.

We have pointed out that the eleven problems covered in 1 Corinthians are of two categories, two groups. To solve the six problems in the first category we need Christ as the unique factor. To solve the five problems in the second category we need the church as the element to settle the matters. Therefore, this book first emphasizes Christ in chapters one through ten, and then it emphasizes the church as the Body of Christ in chapters eleven through sixteen. Therefore, what we see in 1 Corinthians is Christ and the church. Christ is the factor for solving all the problems in the realm of human life, and the church is the element for settling all the problems in the realm of the divine administration. We all need to see Christ in the realm of human life and the church in the realm of the divine administration. (*Life-study of 1 Corinthians*, pp. 463-468)

Further Reading: Life-study of 1 Corinthians, msgs. 52, 55

Enlightenment and inspiration: _____

_____

_____

_____

Morning Nourishment

1 Cor. For he who eats and drinks, eats and drinks
11:29   judgment to himself if he does not discern the
        body.

Eph.   And He subjected all things under His feet and
1:22-23 gave Him *to be* Head over all things to the
        church, which is His Body, the fullness of the
        One who fills all in all.

Although the body in 1 Corinthians 11:24 denotes the physical body of Jesus, Paul uses the expression *not discern the body,* in verse 29 to denote also the mystical Body.

The physical body of Jesus was given on the cross to accomplish redemption for us. But that body has nothing to do with God's present administration. It is the mystical Body of Christ, which is thoroughly and absolutely related to God's administration today. Apart from the mystical Body of Christ, God has no way, no means, to carry out His administration. This means that God's administration is being carried out through the mystical Body of Christ. What are we doing on earth as the mystical Body of Christ? We certainly are not working for the accomplishment of redemption, for redemption has been accomplished once for all by the Lord Jesus. Redemption has been fully accomplished by the offering of the physical body of Jesus on the cross. But Christ today has a mystical Body, and this Body is for the carrying out of God's administration. (*Life-study of 1 Corinthians,* p. 481)

Today's Reading

In 1 Corinthians 11:29 Paul goes on to the matter of discerning the body. Those who do not discern the body eat and drink judgment to themselves. To fail to discern the body indicates a failure to take care of the matter of the church. It is utterly wrong to come to the Lord's supper without taking adequate care of the church. The church today is Christ's mystical Body, and Christ Himself is the Head. In His ascension Christ was made the Head over the entire universe. The church produced by His death is now the mystical Body of this Head.

Because as human beings we have a physical body, we are able to do many things. If we did not have a body, we could not carry on certain activities. In the same principles, the mystical Body of Christ, the church, is for Christ's move on earth. Yes, the Head has gone away, but the Body remains on earth. The Head is now operating God's administration through the Body.

It is a fact of history that the Body has been divided and paralyzed. Even at the time Paul wrote this Epistle, the expression of the Body in Corinth had been divided. This is the reason in chapter eleven he speaks of divisions and parties (vv. 18-19). This indicates that the Body had become ill. Some among the Corinthian believers had become sick and others had died, simply because the Body had been divided (v. 30). They had failed to discern the Body. They did not take care of the Body adequately. From this we must learn the need to take care of the Body, the church. Furthermore, the church bridges the gap between the Lord's first coming and His second coming. This bridge is also a highway from Christ's death to God's kingdom. Without this bridge with the highway, there would be no way to go from one side of the gap, Christ's death, to the other side, God's kingdom. The unique connection is the church as the bridge. Therefore, we must discern the body. This means that we should never damage the bridge. However, many of today's Christians neglect the bridge, and others have damaged it. (*Life-study of 1 Corinthians,* pp. 502-503)

Further Reading: Life-study of 1 Corinthians, msgs. 54, 56

Enlightenment and inspiration: _____

_____

_____

_____

Morning Nourishment

1 Cor. 12:25 That there would be no division in the body, but *that* the members would have the same care for one another.

Eph. 4:3 Being diligent to keep the oneness of the Spirit in the uniting bond of peace.

13 Until we all arrive at the oneness of the faith and of the full knowledge of the Son of God, at a full-grown man, at the measure of the stature of the fullness of Christ.

We have emphasized the fact that when we take the Lord's table we enjoy Him, and when we eat the Lord's supper we satisfy Him by remembering Him and caring for God's administration. But in what way do we take care of this administration? It is by discerning the Body. Many Christians have no idea what it means to discern the Body.

To discern the Body is first to realize that Christ has only one mystical Body. But look at the situation among Christians today. How many divisions there are! Each denomination and group has its own bread. Some even go so far as to insist that if you have not been baptized by them in their water, you will not be allowed to participate in their bread. When we come to the Lord's supper, we must discern the Body to determine whether the bread on the table represents the unique mystical Body of Christ. This is a matter of great importance. (*Life-study of 1 Corinthians,* p. 483)

Today's Reading

The unique mystical Body of Christ is the means for God to carry out His administration. God's eternal purpose is to have a group of saved, redeemed, and regenerated people who have become one to be an organic Body to carry out His administration. But Satan's subtle device is to cut the Body into pieces. This frustrates God's administration. As long as we are in a division, we are through with God's administration. For this reason, today's Christianity has become useless as far as the carrying out of the divine administration is concerned. Christians may preach the gospel to save souls or teach the Bible to help others know the Word. But this is absolutely not adequate to carry out God's administration. The carrying out of the divine administration needs the unique Body, the mystical Body. Because we realize this, we hate division and are absolutely opposed to it.

Divisions damage the mystical Body of Christ with respect to the carrying out of God's administration. Although Christians can preach the gospel and teach the Bible, there are few who care for the mystical Body of Christ for the carrying out of God's administration on earth. Suppose all Christians would care for this. How marvelous this situation would be! What an administration God could have on the earth! But the divisions among Christians not only paralyze the Body of Christ; they even cause the Body to be cut in pieces. This makes it extremely difficult for God to accomplish anything on earth for the carrying out of His administration. For centuries God has not been able to carry out His administration because the unique means for this—the mystical Body of Christ—has been cut into pieces through division.

We must...be impressed that to eat the Lord's supper is to satisfy Him. It is to give Him our remembrance. This implies that we are here for the carrying out of God's administration. In order that God's administration may be carried out, we must care for the oneness of the unique mystical Body of Christ. Having such a concern will preserve us in the Body and keep us from any division. If we have this understanding of the Lord's supper, we shall not be divided by anything. Rather, we shall remain in the unique mystical Body, the means for Christ to carry out His heavenly ministry for the accomplishment of the divine administration. (*Life-study of 1 Corinthians,* pp. 483-485)

Further Reading: Life-study of 1 Corinthians, msgs. 54, 56

Enlightenment and inspiration: _____

_____

_____

_____

Morning Nourishment

1 Cor.   For even as the body is one and has many mem-
12:12-13 bers, yet all the members of the body, being
many, are one body, so also is the Christ. For also
in one Spirit we were all baptized into one Body,
whether Jews or Greeks, whether slaves or free,
and were all given to drink one Spirit.

In the Bible *Christ* sometimes refers to the individual Christ, the personal Christ, and sometimes to the corporate Christ, to Christ and the church (1 Cor. 12:12). The Bible considers Christ and the church as one mysterious Christ. Christ is the Head of this mysterious Christ, and the church is the Body of this mysterious Christ. The two have been joined together to become the one mysterious Christ, a universal great man. All the saved ones in all times and in all space added together become the Body of this mysterious Christ. Individually speaking, we, the saved ones, are particular members of the Body (1 Cor. 12:27). Corporately speaking, we are the mystical Body of Christ. Every saved one is a part of the Body of Christ.

Christ [in 12:12] is not the individual Christ but the corporate Christ, the Body-Christ. In Greek *the Christ* in this verse refers to the corporate Christ, composed of Christ Himself as the Head and the church as His Body with all the believers as its members. All the believers of Christ are organically united with Him and constituted of His life and element to become His Body, an organism, to express Him. Hence, He is not only the Head but also the Body. As our physical body has many members, yet is one, so is this Christ. (*The Conclusion of the New Testament*, p. 2267)

Today's Reading

As a vine includes not only the stalk but also the branches, so the corporate Christ, the Body-Christ, includes not only Christ Himself but also the members of Christ's Body, who are the members of Christ, parts of Christ. According to our natural constitution, we cannot be members of Christ's Body. Christ Himself is the element, the factor, that makes us parts of Him.

Therefore, in order to be parts of Christ, as members of His Body, we must have Christ wrought into our being.

In order to become the corporate Christ, the Body-Christ, Christ had to pass through the steps of a process. First He, the very God, became flesh for our redemption. Then in resurrection He became the life-giving Spirit to come into us and work within us. In this way He becomes the Body-Christ. Now in the church life we enjoy not only God, the Redeemer, and the life-giving Spirit but also the Christ who is the Body.

The church can be the Body of Christ only as the members are constituted of Christ, possessing His life and nature. If we consider our physical body, we shall realize that anything that does not have our life and nature cannot be part of our body. Just as our body is part of us, so Christ's Body, the church, is part of Him. As members of the Body, we are parts of Christ, constituted of Him.

Because the reality of Christ is the Spirit, the way to be constituted of Christ to be His Body is to drink the Spirit. The Body has been formed by the baptism in the one Spirit. In one Spirit we have all been baptized into one Body (1 Cor. 12:13). The baptism into the one Body has positioned us all to drink, and by drinking of the Spirit we are constituted to be the Body. By drinking the Spirit we experience the dispensing of the Divine Trinity into our being and are constituted to be the Body.

The building up of the Body of Christ is altogether a matter of constitution. The Body is an organic entity constituted of the divine element of the processed Triune God. It is through such a constitution that we become the Body of Christ. Therefore, what the Body of Christ needs is not organization but a unique constitution, a constitution which consists of the divine element wrought into our inner being through our drinking of the one Spirit. The more we drink the one Spirit, the more the divine element becomes our constituent to make us the one Body, the corporate Christ. (*The Conclusion of the New Testament,* pp. 2268-2269)

Further Reading: The Conclusion of the New Testament, msgs. 210-212

Enlightenment and inspiration: _____

_____

_____

Morning Nourishment

1 Cor. 12:24-25 But our comely *members* have no need. But God has blended the body together, giving more abundant honor to the *member* that lacked, that there would be no division in the body, but *that* the members would have the same care for one another.

1 John 1:3 That which we have seen and heard we report also to you that you also may have fellowship with us, and indeed our fellowship is with the Father and with His Son Jesus Christ.

In order to be harmonized, blended, adjusted, mingled, and tempered in the Body life, we have to go through the cross and be by the Spirit, dispensing Christ to others for the sake of the Body of Christ. The co-workers and elders must learn to be crossed out. Whatever we do should be by the Spirit to dispense Christ. Also, what we do should not be for our interest and according to our taste but for the church. As long as we practice these points, we will have the blending.

All of these points mean that we should fellowship. When a co-worker does anything, he should fellowship with the other co-workers. An elder should fellowship with the other elders. Fellowship tempers us; fellowship adjusts us; fellowship harmonizes us; and fellowship mingles us....We should not do anything without fellowshipping with the other saints who are coordinating with us. Fellowship requires us to stop when we are about to do something. In our coordination in the church life, in the Lord's work, we all have to learn not to do anything without fellowship. (*The Divine and Mystical Realm*, p. 87)

Today's Reading

Among us we should have the blending of all the individual members of the Body of Christ, the blending of all the churches in certain districts, the blending of all the co-workers, and the blending of all the elders. Blending means that we should always stop to fellowship with others. Then we will receive many benefits. If we isolate and seclude ourselves, we will lose much spiritual profit. Learn to fellowship. Learn to be blended. From now on, the churches should come together frequently to be blended. We may not be used to it, but after we begin to practice blending a few times, we will acquire the taste for it. This is the most helpful thing in the keeping of the oneness of the universal Body of Christ.

When we blend together, we have the cross and the Spirit. Without the cross and the Spirit, all that we have is the flesh with division. It is not easy to be crucified and to do all things by the Spirit in ourselves. This is why we must learn to be blended. Blending requires us to be crossed out. Blending requires us to be by the Spirit to dispense Christ and to do everything for the sake of His Body.

When we come together, we should experience the terminating of the cross. Then we should learn how to follow the Spirit, how to dispense Christ, and how to say and do something for the benefit of the Body. That will change the entire atmosphere of the meeting and will temper the atmosphere. Blending is not a matter of being quiet or talkative but a matter of being tempered. We can be in harmony, because we have been tempered. Eventually, the distinctions will all be gone. Blending means to lose the distinctions. We all have to pay some price to practice the blending.

A group of elders may meet together often without being blended. To be blended means that you are touched by others and that you are touching others. But you should touch others in a blending way. Go through the cross, do things by the Spirit, and do everything to dispense Christ for His Body's sake. We should not come to a blending meeting to be silent. We have to prepare ourselves to say something for the Lord. The Lord may use you, but you need to be tempered and crossed out, and you need to learn how to follow the Spirit to dispense Christ for His Body's sake. (*The Divine and Mystical Realm,* pp. 87-88)

Further Reading: The Divine and Mystical Realm, ch. 6; *The Practical Points concerning Blending,* chs. 1-5*

Enlightenment and inspiration: _____

_____

_____

_____

Morning Nourishment

1 Cor. 1:2 To the church of God which is in Corinth...

7:17 ...And so I direct in all the churches.

11:16 ...We do not have such a custom *of being so,* neither the churches of God.

12:27 Now you are the Body of Christ, and members individually.

14:33 ...As in all the churches of the saints.

Eph. 2:22 In whom you also are being built together into a dwelling place of God in spirit.

4:4 One Body and one Spirit...

Rev. 1:11 Saying, What you see write in a scroll and send *it* to the seven churches...

For the Lord's move in His recovery both locally and universally, we all need to be Body-conscious in one accord and Body-centered in oneness. In one accord we should be Body-conscious. In oneness we should be Body-centered. In our consideration the Body should be first and the local churches should be second. The United States becomes the top country on this earth, not because of the autonomy of its states, but because of the unity of all the states. What a shame it is for any local church to declare its autonomy! To teach that the local churches are absolutely autonomous is to divide the Body of Christ. All the local churches are and should be one Body universally, doctrinally, and practically. Otherwise, where is the unique church of God and the unique one new man for the fulfilling of God's economy?! (*One Body and One Spirit,* p. 24)

Today's Reading

The one Body is the one church of God (Eph. 1:22; 1 Cor. 10:32b), manifested in many localities (Rev. 1:11) as many local churches (v. 4)....The local churches are many in existence but are still one Body universally in element (Eph. 4:4). In existence the churches are many....However, in element all the churches are one. We are one church, one Body, one new man. In element we are not divided, and we cannot be autonomous.

The secret of the practice of the church life is first the one accord in the local churches. Second, the secret of the practice of the church life is the oneness in the universal Body (Eph. 4:3; John 17:11, 21-23). Some insist to say, "We are local churches. Every local church has its own jurisdiction. Don't touch our affairs. If you touch our affairs, you touch our local administration." To say such a word is to make all the local churches separate from one another. This is separation; this is not oneness. Oneness should be among the local churches, and one accord should be in every local church. Then we will have the blessing....If we would all be in the oneness universally and in the one accord locally, the meeting halls of all the churches would be filled.

All the local churches on the globe today should be one. Today, unlike in Paul's time, travel and communication to nearly anywhere on the earth are very convenient. Because of this, the churches today should be blended much more than they were in Paul's time. Not only according to the revelation of the Bible but also according to the modern conveniences, we should be one, and we should be blended together as much as practicality allows.

All the local churches should be absolutely one in the realm of five crucial things: (1) the growth of life for the testimony of Jesus Christ; (2) the preaching of the gospel; (3) the spreading of the Lord's recovery; (4) the building up of the Body of Christ; and (5) the accomplishment of God's eternal economy. We should be one in all these things.

We do not need to be one in certain things concerning the administration of the church....But in the growth of life for the testimony of the Lord, in the preaching of the gospel, in the spreading of the Lord's recovery, in the building up of the Body of Christ, and in the accomplishment of God's eternal economy, we have to be one universally. (*One Body and One Spirit*, pp. 17-20, 23)

Further Reading: One Body and One Spirit, ch. 1; The Practical Points concerning Blending, chs. 1-4; A Genuine Church; The Conclusion of the New Testament, msg. 200

Enlightenment and inspiration: _____
_____
_____
_____

Hymns, #819

1 As the body is the fulness
   To express our life,
   So to Christ the Church, His Body,
   Doth express His life.

2 E'en as Eve is part of Adam
   Taken out of him,
   So the Church is Christ's own increase
   With Himself within.

3 As from out the buried kernel
   Many grains are formed,
   As the grains together blended
   To a loaf are formed;

4 So the Church, of many Christians,
   Christ doth multiply,
   Him expressing as one Body,
   God to glorify.

5 As the branches of the grapevine
   Are its outward spread,
   With it one, abiding, bearing
   Clusters in its stead;

6 So the Church's many members
   Christ's enlargement are,
   One with Him in life and living,
   Spreading Him afar.

7 Fulness, increase, duplication,
   His expression full,
   Growth and spread, continuation,
   Surplus plentiful,

8 Is the Church to Christ, and thereby
   God in Christ may be
   Glorified thru His redeemed ones
   To eternity.

9   Thus the Church and Christ together,
     God's great mystery,
    Is the mingling of the Godhead
    With humanity.

Composition for prophecy with main point and sub-points: _____

_____
_____
_____
_____
_____
_____
_____
_____
_____
_____
_____
_____
_____
_____
_____
_____
_____
_____
_____
_____
_____
_____
_____
_____
_____
_____
_____
_____
_____
_____
_____

The Most Excellent Way
for the Building Up of the Church

Scripture Reading: 1 Cor. 8:1; 12:31b—14:1; 16:24

Day 1

I. Love is the most excellent way for the building up of the church, and prophesying is the excelling gift for the building up of the church (1 Cor. 8:1; 12:31b—14:1, 4b, 12):

A. Paul's ultimate concern is the building up of the church, which is the primary thing in God's economy (Matt. 16:18).

B. To take the way of love and to prophesy (to speak the Lord into others) are to enter into the contents of God's entire New Testament economy, which is Christ as the Son of Man cherishing us and as the Son of God nourishing us (Eph. 5:29).

Day 2

II. Love is the most excellent way to use the gifts, the way to be in the Body, and the way to be for the Body (1 Cor. 12:31b—13:13):

A. God is love; we love because He first loved us (1 John 4:8, 19).

B. God's predestination of us unto the divine sonship was motivated by the divine love (Eph. 1:4-5).

C. God's giving of His only begotten Son to us that we may be saved from perdition judicially through His death and have the eternal life organically in His resurrection was motivated by the divine love (John 3:16; 1 John 4:9-10).

D. God's love motivates us, His children, to love our enemies that we may be perfect as He is; He loves the fallen human race, who became His enemies, by causing His sun (signifying Christ) to rise on the evil and the good indiscriminately and by sending rain (signifying

the Spirit) on the just and the unjust equally;
thus, we may become the sons of the heavenly
Father who are sanctified from the tax collectors and the Gentiles (Matt. 5:43-48).

Day 3

E. "Knowledge puffs up, but love builds up"
(1 Cor. 8:1):

1. The outward, objective knowledge that
puffs up comes from the tree of the
knowledge of good and evil, the source of
death.

2. The spiritual, not fleshly, love, which is
an expression of life as described in
1 Corinthians 13, builds up; it comes from
the tree of life, the source of life.

3. This is the love of God (1 John 4:16) infused
into us by faith, which has brought us into
the organic union with God.

4. By this love we love God (1 Cor. 8:3) and
the brothers (1 John 4:21), and according
to this love we should walk (Rom. 14:15);
thus, our walk builds up (1 Cor. 10:23).

5. This building up refers not only to the edification of individual believers but also to
the building up of the corporate Body of
Christ (14:4-5, 12; 3:9-10, 12; 10:23; Eph.
4:16).

6. "If anyone loves God, this one is known by
Him" (1 Cor. 8:3):

a. Loving God is the base of our Christian
life; it must be spiritual, not fleshly,
although it requires the exercise of
man's entire being (Mark 12:30; cf. 1 Cor.
16:22):

1) Our loving God makes us those who
are blessed of God to share the divine
blessings that He has ordained and
prepared for us (Christ as the depths
of God), which are beyond our appre-
hension (2:9-10).

Day 4

Day 5

   2) Our not loving the Lord makes us those who are accursed, set apart to a curse (16:22).

   b. To be known by God is to be owned and possessed by Him as His treasure; the one who is known by God becomes God's possession, joy, entertainment, and pleasure (cf. Col. 1:10).

   c. To say that God does not know you means that He does not approve of your way (Matt. 7:22-23).

F. "Love suffers long. Love is kind; it is not jealous. Love does not brag and is not puffed up; it does not behave unbecomingly and does not seek its own things; it is not provoked and does not take account of evil; it does not rejoice because of unrighteousness, but rejoices with the truth; it covers all things, believes all things, hopes all things, endures all things. Love never falls away" (1 Cor. 13:4-8a).

G. Love is the conclusion of all spiritual virtues and the factor of fruit-bearing that supplies us bountifully with the rich entrance into the kingdom of Christ (2 Pet. 1:5-11).

H. The Body of Christ builds itself up in love (Eph. 4:16).

I. The spirit that God gives us is of love; hence, it is of power and sobermindedness (2 Tim. 1:7).

J. He who does not love abides in death (1 John 3:14b).

K. We must pursue love while we desire spiritual gifts (1 Cor. 14:1).

L. To overcome the degradation of the church we need to pursue love with those who call on the Lord out of a pure heart (2 Tim. 2:22).

M. Loving one another is a sign that we belong to Christ (John 13:34-35).

N. The love of God makes us more than conquerors over our circumstantial situations (Rom. 8:35-39).

Day 6   **III. The genuine love is the issue of the enjoyment of God in His divine nature (2 Pet. 1:4):**

   A. The divine nature is what God is; God is Spirit (John 4:24), love (1 John 4:8, 16), and light (1:5); Spirit is the nature of God's person, love is the nature of God's essence, and light is the nature of God's expression.

   B. We can enjoy God as love in our fellowship with Him (vv. 2-3):

     1. If we remain in the divine fellowship to enjoy what God is as love in His essence, we will be bathed in the love of God; we will not only become a man of love, but we will become love itself.

     2. This love should saturate us until it becomes the love with which we love the brothers; the Lord desires a church of such brotherly love (Rev. 3:7a).

     3. Paul ends 1 Corinthians with a word of the assurance of love; this is not a natural love but love in Christ, love in resurrection (4:21), the love of God that becomes ours through the grace of Christ and the fellowship of the Spirit (16:24; 2 Cor. 13:14).

Morning Nourishment

Eph. For no one ever hated his own flesh, but nourishes
5:29 and cherishes it, even as Christ also the church.
Matt. ...He said, Those who are strong have no need of a
9:12 physician, but those who are ill.
1 Cor. ...And moreover I show to you a most excellent
12:31 way.
13:7-8 [Love] covers all things....Love never falls *away*....
14:1 Pursue love...
8:1 ...Knowledge puffs up, but love builds up.

The full ministry of Christ is in three stages: incarnation, inclusion, and intensification. His ministry in the first stage of incarnation was to cherish people, to draw and attract people to Him....His visiting was His cherishing. His death on the cross was the biggest cherishing to redeem us. Without His redemption, who could come to Him? When we heard the story of His death on the cross, our tears came down. We were attracted by Him. This is His ministry in the four Gospels.

In resurrection He was transfigured to become the life-giving Spirit, the Spirit of the bountiful supply (1 Cor. 15:45b; Phil. 1:19). This Spirit is for nourishing....This nourishing produces the church, builds up the Body of Christ, and will consummate the New Jerusalem. Because of the church's degradation, Christ's nourishing becomes sevenfold intensified in the book of Revelation to bring forth the eternal goal of God, the New Jerusalem,...which is the enlargement and expression of God....The New Testament is composed of just two sections—cherishing and nourishing. (*The Vital Groups,* p. 82)

Today's Reading

The end of 1 Corinthians 12 reveals that love is the most excellent way (v. 31b)....How do we shepherd people? Love is the most excellent way. Love is the most excellent way for us to prophesy and to teach others. Love is the most excellent way for us to be anything or do anything.

Love prevails. We should love everybody, even our enemies.

If the co-workers and elders do not love the bad ones, eventually they will have nothing to do. We must be perfect as our Father is perfect (Matt. 5:48) by loving the evil ones and the good ones without any discrimination. We must be perfect as our Father because we are His sons, His species. This is most crucial....We must love any kind of person. The Lord Jesus said that He came to be a Physician, not for the healthy ones, but for the sick ones...(Matt. 9:12).

The church is not a police station to arrest people or a law court to judge people, but a home to raise up the believers. Parents know that the worse their children are, the more they need their raising up. If our children were angels, they would not need our parenting to raise them up. The church is a loving home to raise up the children. The church is also a hospital to heal and to recover the sick ones. Finally, the church is a school to teach and edify the unlearned ones who do not have much understanding. Because the church is a home, a hospital, and a school, the co-workers and elders should be one with the Lord to raise up, to heal, to cover, and to teach others in love.

Some of the churches, however, are police stations to arrest the sinful ones and law courts to judge them. Paul's attitude was different. He said, "Who is weak, and I am not weak?" (2 Cor. 11:29a). When the scribes and Pharisees brought an adulterous woman to the Lord, He said to them, "He who is without sin among you, let him be the first to throw a stone at her" (John 8:7). After all of them left,...Jesus said, "Neither do I condemn you" (vv. 10-11). Who is without sin? Who is perfect? Paul said, "To the weak I became weak that I might gain the weak" (1 Cor. 9:22). This is love. We should not consider that others are weak but we are not. This is not love. Love covers and builds up, so love is the most excellent way for us to be anything and to do anything for the building up of the Body of Christ. (*The Vital Groups,* pp. 74-75)

Further Reading: The Vital Groups, msgs. 8-9; *Life-study of 1 Corinthians,* msg. 61; *How to Meet,* ch. 9

Enlightenment and inspiration: _____

_____

_____

_____

Morning Nourishment

1 John 4:8	He who does not love has not known God, because God is love.
John 3:16	For God so loved the world that He gave His only begotten Son, that every one who believes into Him would not perish, but would have eternal life.
Matt. 5:44-45	But I say to you, Love your enemies, and pray for those who persecute you, so that you may become sons of your Father who is in the heavens, because He causes His sun to rise on the evil and the good and sends rain on the just and the unjust.

We are God's species because we have been born of Him to have His life and nature (John 1:12-13). We have been regenerated to be God's species, God's kind, and God is love. Since we become God in His life and nature, we also should be love. This means that we do not merely love others but that we are love itself. As His species we should be love because He is love. Whoever is love is God's species, God's kind.

God is love; we love because He first loved us (1 John 4:8, 19). God does not want us to love with our natural love but with Him as our love. God created man in His image (Gen. 1:26),...according to His attributes, the first of which is love. Although created man does not have the reality of love, there is something in his created being that wants to love others. Even fallen man has the desire to love within him. But that is just a human virtue, the very expression of the divine attribute of love. When we were regenerated, God infused us with Himself as love. We love Him because He first loved us. He initiated this love. (*The Vital Groups,* p. 69)

Today's Reading

God's predestination of us unto the divine sonship was motivated by the divine love. Ephesians 1:4-5 says that God chose us in Christ before the foundation of the world "to be holy and without blemish before Him in love, predestinating us unto sonship." The phrase *in love* can be joined with the phrase *predestinating us unto sonship.* God predestinated us unto sonship in love.

God's giving of His only begotten Son to us that we may be saved from perdition judicially through His death and have the eternal life organically in His resurrection was motivated by the divine love (John 3:16; 1 John 4:9-10). John 3:16 is strengthened by two verses from John's first Epistle—4:9 and 10. First John 4:10 says that God sent His Son to us as a propitiation for our sins. This is judicial through His death. Verse 9 says that God sent His Son to us that we may have life and live through Him. This is organic in His resurrection.

God's love motivates us, His children, to love our enemies that we may be perfect as He is; He loves the fallen human race, who became His enemies, by causing His sun (signifying Christ) to rise on the evil and the good indiscriminately and sending rain (signifying the Spirit) on the just and the unjust equally; thus, we may become the sons of the heavenly Father who are sanctified from the tax collectors and the Gentiles (Matt. 5:43-48). The entire human race became His enemies, but God still loves the human race. If God sent Christ to us with discrimination, we would be disqualified from receiving His salvation. He causes His sun to rise first on the evil and then on the good without discrimination.

We should be like God in our love for others....If we love only those who love us, we are of the same species as the tax collectors [v. 46]. But we are of the super, divine species, so we love the evil ones, our enemies, as well as the good ones. This shows how God as love prevails.

The vital groups should be...prevailing. A proof that our vital group is prevailing is that we love people without any discrimination....[Consider the fact that] the first one saved by Christ through His crucifixion was not a gentleman, but a criminal, a robber, sentenced to death. This is very meaningful. (*The Vital Groups,* pp. 69-71)

Further Reading: The Vital Groups, msg. 8; *A Word of Love to the Co-workers, Elders, Lovers, and Seekers of the Lord,* ch. 2

Enlightenment and inspiration: _____

_____

_____

_____

Morning Nourishment

1 Cor.   Now concerning things sacrificed to idols, we
8:1-3   know that we all have knowledge. Knowledge
         puffs up, but love builds up. If anyone thinks that
         he knows anything, he has not yet come to know
         as he ought to know; but if anyone loves God, this
         one is known by Him.
Matt.   And then I will declare to them: I never knew you.
7:23   Depart from Me, you workers of lawlessness.

In 1 Corinthians 8...two Greek words are used for know. One
is *oida* (vv. 1, 4), signifying the inward, subjective consciousness,
the intuitive knowledge....The other is *ginosko* (vv. 2-3), signifying
the outward, objective knowledge. The word knowledge in verse 1
and in verses 7 and 10 is the noun form of *ginosko*, referring to the
outward, objective knowledge, which is common and general to all.
   The outward, objective knowledge that puffs up comes from the
tree of knowledge of good and evil, the source of death. The spiritual,
not fleshly, love, which is an expression of life as described in chapter
thirteen, builds up. It comes from the tree of life, the source of life.
This is the love of God (1 John 4:16) infused into us by faith
which has brought us into the organic union with God. By this
love we love God (1 Cor. 8:3) and the brothers (1 John 4:21), and
according to this love we should walk (Rom. 14:15). Thus, our
walk builds up (1 Cor. 10:23). The expression *builds up* in this
verse refers not only to the edification of individual believers,
but also to the building up of the corporate Body of Christ
(14:4-5, 12; Eph. 4:16). This book stresses the matter of building
up (3:9-10, 12; 10:23). (*Life-study of 1 Corinthians*, p. 387)

Today's Reading

   The knowledge which puffs up and the love which builds up
are related to the two trees in the garden of Eden....In this book
these two trees are illustrated, although there is no direct
mention of them. Actually 1 Corinthians deals with the tree of
life which supplies life and the tree of knowledge which kills.
Thus, in this book there are two lines, the line of life and the line

of knowledge. Knowledge puffs up and even kills, but love supplies life and builds up others with life. Life is for the building,
and the building is accomplished by life....In [8:2 and 3] the Greek
word for know is *ginosko*. The love spoken of in verse 3 is the
highest and noblest love. It must be spiritual, not fleshly, although it involves the exercise of man's entire being (Mark 12:30).

Loving God is the base of our Christian life. If we do not have
such a love, we do not have the standing, the base, for the
Christian life. As far as the Christian life is concerned, knowledge
is like a vapor; it can disappear quickly. Loving God, however, is
solid and substantial. Hence, it is the base of the Christian life.

In verse 3 Paul says that if we love God, we are known by Him.
It is more necessary for us to be known by God than for us to know
God....To be known by God means to be owned and possessed by
Him. The one who is known by God becomes God's possession, joy,
entertainment, and pleasure. Our knowledge does not please
God. But if we love God,...He will know us, enjoy us, and be
happy with us....All this is implied by the words *known by Him*.

In verse 3 Paul seems to be telling the Corinthians, "You
believers at Corinth need to realize that God does not know you.
He is not pleased with you. To say that God does not know you
means that He does not approve of your way." According to
Matthew 7:22, many will say to the Lord Jesus at the time of
His coming again, "Lord, did we not prophesy in Your name,
and in Your name cast out demons, and in Your name do many
works of power?" The Lord will answer, "I never knew you.
Depart from Me, you workers of lawlessness" (v. 23)....I never
knew you in Matthew 7:23 means, "I never approved of what
you have done. I was never happy with you or took you as my
joy and treasure." To be known by God implies that He approves
of us, enjoys us, and possesses us as a treasure. (*Life-study of
1 Corinthians*, pp. 387-389)

Further Reading: Life-study of 1 Corinthians, msg. 44; *The
Practical Expression of the Church,* chs. 1, 3-5*

Enlightenment and inspiration: _____

_____
_____
_____

Morning Nourishment

1 Cor. Love suffers long. Love is kind; it is not jealous.
13:4-8 Love does not brag and is not puffed up; it does not
behave unbecomingly and does not seek its own
things; it is not provoked and does not take account
of evil; it does not rejoice because of unrighteousness, but rejoices with the truth; it covers all things,
believes all things, hopes all things, endures all
things. Love never falls away. But whether prophecies, they will be rendered useless; or tongues, they
will cease; or knowledge, it will be rendered useless.

Love is the expression of life, which is the element of God.
Hence, God is love (1 John 4:16). God as life is expressed in love.
All the fifteen virtues of love listed in [1 Corinthians 13:4-7] are
the divine virtues of God's life. Such a life differs from the
outward gifts listed in chapter twelve. The Corinthians were
after the outward gifts, but they neglected love, the expression
of life. Thus, they were still fleshy, fleshly, or soulish (3:1, 3; 2:14).
They needed to grow in life, expressed by love, by pursuing love,
not the outward gifts, so that they might be spiritual (2:14).

In verse 4 Paul says that love does not brag. Bragging is
somewhat different from boasting. To brag is to boast of one's self
in a way to damage others. It is a kind of boasting which depreciates
others and puts them down. Love certainly does not brag.

In verse 5 Paul points out that love "does not take account of
evil." The Greek word here indicates that love does not keep a record
like a bookkeeper. This means that if you love others, you will not
keep a record of their mistakes. (*Life-study of 1 Corinthians*, p. 539)

Today's Reading

First Corinthians 13:6 says, "[Love] does not rejoice because of
unrighteousness, but rejoices with the truth." The totality of unrighteousness is Satan, and the totality of truth is God. Love as the
expression of the divine life does not rejoice over Satan's unrighteousness, but rejoices with God's truth. Love does not rejoice
over anyone's unrighteousness; instead, it rejoices with the truth.

Love covers all things [v. 7]. The Greek word [for *covers*]...means "to contain (as a vessel)," "to conceal", hence, "to cover (as a roof)." This word is used in the Gospels regarding the incident where some people broke up a roof in order to bring a certain sick man to the Lord Jesus. They made a hole in the roof and then lowered the man to the place where the Lord was (Mark 2:4). This Greek word means to make a hole in someone's roof. We may do this by gossiping about others. As we talk about them, we make a hole in the roof over them; that is, we uncover them. However, love covers all things; it does not make a hole in anyone's roof.

If we consider the fifteen virtues of love listed in these verses, we shall realize that love is nothing other than God Himself. Who other than God could have all these virtues?...God is love (1 John 4:16). God is also life. Life is God's essence, and love is God's expression. In Himself God is life, but God expressed is love. The love which is God Himself with His divine essence as life has these fifteen virtues. This is the reason that in 1 Corinthians Paul charges the believers to grow in life. They were short of life, short of love. In other words, they were short of God and needed to grow in life.

In 13:8-13 Paul speaks concerning the excelling of love. In verse 8,...for love never to fall away means that it survives everything, holds its place forever. Love never fails, never fades out or comes to an end. It is like the eternal life of God. All the gifts, whether prophecies, or tongues, or knowledge, are means for God's operation; they are not life to express God. Hence, they shall cease and be done away. They are all dispensational. Only life, which love expresses, is eternal. According to the following verses, all gifts are for the immature child in this age. They will all be done away in the next age. Only love is of a mature man and will last for eternity. When we live and act by love, we have a foretaste of the next age and of eternity. (*Life-study of 1 Corinthians,* pp. 539-541)

Further Reading: Life-study of 1 Corinthians, msg. 60; *How to Meet,* ch. 9; *A Word of Love to the Co-workers, Elders, Lovers, and Seekers of the Lord,* ch. 2

Enlightenment and inspiration: _____

_____

_____

_____

Morning Nourishment

Eph. Out from whom all the Body...causes the growth
4:16 of the Body unto the building up of itself in love.

2 Tim. For God has not given us a spirit of cowardice, but
1:7 of power and of love and of sobermindedness.

2:22 But flee youthful lusts, and pursue righteousness,
faith, love, peace with those who call on the Lord
out of a pure heart.

1 John We know that we have passed out of death into life
3:14 because we love the brothers. He who does not
love abides in death.

Love is the conclusion of all spiritual virtues and the factor
of fruit-bearing that supplies us bountifully with the rich entrance into the kingdom of Christ (2 Pet. 1:5-11).

The Body of Christ builds itself up in love (Eph. 4:16). The
phrase *in love* is used repeatedly in the book of Ephesians (1:4;
3:17; 4:2, 15-16; 5:2). God predestinated us unto sonship before
the foundation of the world in love, and the Body of Christ builds
itself up in love. The growth in life is in love. In the last few
years we have appreciated the Lord's showing us the high peak
of the divine revelation. My concern is that although we may
talk about the truths of the high peak, love is absent among us.
If this is the case, we are puffed up, not built up. The Body of
Christ builds itself up in love. (*The Vital Groups,* pp. 72-73)

Today's Reading

The spirit that God has given us is our human spirit regenerated and indwelt by the Holy Spirit. This spirit is a spirit of
love; hence, it is of power and of sobermindedness (2 Tim. 1:7).
We may think that we are very powerful and sober, but our
spirit is not of love. We talk to people in a way that is full of
power and sobermindedness, but our talk threatens them.

Paul said that we need to fan our gift into flame (v. 6). The
main gift which God has given us is our regenerated human
spirit with His Spirit, His life, and His nature. We must fan this
gift into flame. This means that we have to stir up our spirit so

that our spirit will be burning. Romans 12:11 says that we should be burning in spirit. If our spirit is not a spirit of love, our fanning it into flame will burn the whole recovery in a negative way. We must have a burning spirit of love, not a burning spirit of authority which damages. Whatever is mentioned in 2 Timothy is a requirement for us to face the degradation of the church. How can we overcome the degradation of the church? We must have a burning human spirit of love. Under today's degradation of the church, we all need a spirit of love fanned into flame to be burning in spirit. Love prevails in this way.

According to my observation throughout the years, most of the co-workers have a human spirit of "power" but not of love. We need a spirit of love to conquer the degradation of today's church. We should not say or do anything to threaten people. Instead we should always say and do things with a spirit of love, which has been fanned into flame. This is what the recovery needs.

First John 3:14b says that he who does not love abides in death. We may think that we are living, but we are dead because we do not love. If we do not love our brother, we abide in death and are dead, but if we do love him, we abide in life and are living.

First Corinthians 13 speaks of love, and then chapter fourteen begins by saying that we are to pursue love while we desire spiritual gifts (v. 1). Our desiring of gifts must go along with the pursuing of love. Otherwise, the gifts will puff us up.

To overcome the degradation of the church we need to pursue love with those who seek the Lord out of a pure heart (2 Tim. 2:22). We have to pursue love with a group of seekers of the Lord. This is a vital group.

Loving one another is a sign that we belong to Christ (John 13:34-35). We do not need to bear an outward sign....If all the saints in the Lord's recovery love one another, the whole world will say that these people are of Christ. (*The Vital Groups,* pp. 73-74)

Further Reading: The Vital Groups, msg. 8; *The Practical Expression of the Church,* chs. 1, 3-5*

Enlightenment and inspiration: _____

_____

_____

_____

Morning Nourishment

2 Pet. Through which He has granted to us precious and
1:4 exceedingly great promises that through these
you might become partakers of the divine nature,
having escaped the corruption which is in the
world by lust.

1 John And we know and have believed the love which
4:16 God has in us. God is love, and he who abides in
love abides in God and God abides in him.

1:3 That which we have seen and heard we report also
to you that you also may have fellowship with us,
and indeed our fellowship is with the Father and
with His Son Jesus Christ.

We believers have all been made partakers of this divine nature (2 Pet. 1:4). It is a very hard task to define the divine nature. Simply speaking, the divine nature is what God is, just as the nature of anything is what that thing is. We have seen that the Bible tells us that God is Spirit (John 4:24), that God is love (1 John 4:8, 16), and that God is light (1 John 1:5). Then in a total way the Bible tells us that God is life (John 1:4; 5:26; 14:6). These four items of what God is are very basic. Spirit, love, and light are the very constituents of God's being and life is God Himself. God Himself, God's being, is our life and He is constituted with Spirit, love, and light. Spirit is the nature of God's Person, love is the nature of God's essence, and light is the nature of God's expression.

God is Spirit in person, God is love in essence, God is light in expression, and God is life in love as its essence and in light as its expression. When we touch God, we touch Him as Spirit in His Person, as love in His essence, and as light in His expression. After touching God, we walk, we live, we have our being, in His Spirit as our person, in His love as our essence, and in His light as our expression.

If you remain in the divine fellowship to enjoy not only what God gives or what God does for you but also what God is as love in His essence and as light in His expression, you will be bathed in the love of God. You will become not only a man of love, but you will become love itself. (*God's New Testament Economy*, pp. 331, 344)

Today's Reading

Let us consider our set-apart time to fellowship with the
Lord. In such a fellowship you realize and enjoy the Lord as the
Spirit, and simultaneously you enjoy the nature of God's essence, which is love. Love then saturates you and even becomes
you. Before this time, you may have been disgusted with...your
wife,...but afterwards you are filled with love for your wife. This
love has not only filled you but saturated you. The reason why
we Christians can love persons whom others cannot love is
because we enjoy God as love. We enjoy the divine nature of this
loving God. This is why John tells us in his first Epistle that if
we love our brother this means we are born of God because God
is love (4:7-8). When you love others you are enjoying the divine
nature....Only those who partake of the divine nature love
people genuinely. They are not taught to love others, but they
have become love toward others. They are the partakers of the
divine love, which is the very nature of the divine essence.

Ephesians 5:25 charges the husbands to love their wives. A
certain husband may feel that since his wife is not so lovable,
he could not love her. Furthermore, he may think that if his
wife were like another sister, he would love her. Even if another
sister were married to this brother, however, he would still not
be satisfied. What he needs to experience is the nobler love. Our
poor human love is always short. To say or to think that you
cannot love your wife proves that you have not partaken of the
divine nature to the extent that you are experiencing and
enjoying the divine love. If you have partaken of the divine
nature to such an extent, you would love any kind of wife. A
nobler love does not exercise any kind of choice. (*God's New
Testament Economy,* pp. 328-329, 339-340)

Further Reading: God's New Testament Economy, chs. 30-32;
    Life-study of 1 Corinthians, msg. 69

Enlightenment and inspiration: _____

_____

_____

_____

Hymns, #30

1   What love Thou hast bestowed on us,
      We thank Thee from our heart;
      Our Father, we would worship Thee
      And praise for all Thou art.

2   Thy heart Thou hast revealed to us,
      Made known th' eternal will;
      Within the Son Thou hast come forth,
      Thy purpose to fulfill.

3   Thou gavest Thy beloved Son
      In love to come and die,
      That we may be Thy many sons,
      As heirs with Him, made nigh.

4   Through Him we have Thy very life
      And Thou our Father art;
      Thy very nature, all Thyself,
      Thou dost to us impart.

5   Thy Spirit into ours has come
      That we may "Abba" cry;
      Of Spirit born, with Spirit sealed,
      To be transformed thereby.

6   The many sons to glory brought
      Is Thine eternal goal,
      And to Thy Son's own image wrought,
      Thou wilt conform the whole.

7   Throughout Thy transformation work
      Thou dost direct each one,
      From glory unto glory bring
      Until the work is done.

8   What love Thou, Father, hast bestowed;
      We'll ever grateful be;
      We'll worship Thee forevermore
      And praise unceasingly.

Composition for prophecy with main point and sub-points: _____

The Excelling Gift
for the Building Up of the Church

Scripture Reading: 1 Cor. 14:1, 3-5, 12, 24-26, 31-32, 37, 39

Day 1 I. **Prophesying is the excelling gift produced in the growth in life through the enjoyment of Christ for the building up of the church (v. 12; Matt. 16:18; 1 Cor. 14:4b).**

II. **Prophesying in 1 Corinthians 14 is not in the sense of predicting, foretelling, but in the sense of speaking for the Lord, speaking forth the Lord, to dispense Christ into people (vv. 1, 12, 39a):**

A. Prophesying is to speak to men building up for the church, encouragement for the believers, and consolation for the saints' spiritual welfare (v. 3; cf. 3:12).

B. Prophesying convicts people, judges people, and exposes the secrets of people's hearts (14:23-25).

C. Prophesying is for the building up of the church, which is the organism of the Triune God, in the way of life (vv. 4-5).

III. **God's desire is for all of His saints to prophesy (Num. 11:29; 1 Cor. 14:31).**

Day 2 IV. **Prophesying is the excelling gift among all the gifts, making its seekers excelling (v. 12):**

A. Prophesying is excelling in revealing God's heart, God's will, God's way, and God's economy to His people (cf. 12:8).

B. Prophesying is excelling in convicting people, exposing people's real condition, and showing people their spiritual need.

C. Prophesying is excelling in speaking forth Christ to minister and dispense Christ to people for their nourishment.

D. Prophesying is excelling in building up the church in the organic way that it may be built up as the organism of the processed Triune God for His fullness, His expression.

Day 3 V. **All the believers have the capacity, the ability, to prophesy, and all have the obligation to prophesy (14:31, 24):**

A. The capacity to prophesy is in the divine life, which the believers possess and enjoy and which needs to increase within them so that this capacity may be developed unto their ability (Col. 2:19; cf. 2 Tim. 4:5).

B. The obligation to prophesy is the fulfillment of our spiritual service, in which we are indebted to God's salvation (Rom. 1:14-15).

Day 4 VI. **All the believers have been charged by the apostle to pursue, to seek, and to desire earnestly to prophesy (1 Cor. 14:1, 12, 39a):**

A. We are enabled to prophesy by learning (v. 31) in the Word of God, in the growth of life, and in our contact with God (2 Tim. 3:16-17; 1 Thes. 5:17-20; Gal. 5:16, 25):

1. We need to be revived every morning (Prov. 4:18; Lam. 3:22-24; Psa. 119:147-148).

2. We need to live an overcoming life every day by calling on the Lord's name in every place and living in the index of His eyes (1 Cor. 1:2; 12:3b; 2 Cor. 2:10).

3. To live an overcoming life is to live a prophesying life by loving the Lord to the uttermost (1 Cor. 2:9), fellowshipping with Him moment by moment (cf. 1 John 1:6), walking according to the spirit (Rom. 8:4b), and speaking the word of the Lord in season and out of season (2 Tim. 4:2a).

B. We are enabled to prophesy by being perfected by the prophets (Eph. 4:11-12).

C. We are enabled to prophesy by practicing to speak in all the meetings and by telling people about Christ (1 Cor. 14:26; Phil. 2:16a; 2 Tim. 4:2a, 5).

Day 5   **VII. In order to practice 1 Corinthians 14, there is the need for the highest meetings of the church, meetings in which "each one has" (v. 26):**

     A. The proper church meeting is a "one another" meeting, a "round table" meeting, in which we speak to one another (Eph. 5:19), teach and admonish one another (Col. 3:16), consider one another and exhort one another (Heb. 10:24-25), and listen to one another (1 Thes. 5:20).

     B. The proper church meeting makes the believers living by developing their organic ability and function (Eph. 4:16).

     C. Before coming to the meeting, we should prepare ourselves for the meeting through our experience of the Lord or through our enjoyment of His word and fellowship with Him in prayer.

     D. After coming into the meeting, we need not wait, and should not wait, for inspiration; we should exercise our spirit and use our trained mind to function in presenting what we have prepared to the Lord for His glory and satisfaction and to the attendants for their benefit—their enlightenment, nourishing, and building up.

     E. We must labor on Christ, our good land, so that we may reap some produce of His riches to bring to the church meeting and offer to God (Deut. 16:16).

     F. Thus, the meeting will be an exhibition of Christ in His riches and will be a mutual enjoyment of Christ shared by all the attendants before God and with God for the building up of the saints and the church.

Day 6   **VIII. We must speak with the three constituting elements of prophesying:**

     A. We must possess a knowledge of the Word of God—the human element of learning (2 Tim. 3:16-17; Ezek. 3:1-4).

B. We must have the instant inspiration of the Holy Spirit—the divine element of inspiration (1 Cor. 14:32, 37a; 1 John 1:6-7; Rom. 8:4).

C. We must have a vision concerning God's interest and economy, concerning the church as the Body of Christ, concerning the local churches, concerning the world, concerning the individual saints, and even concerning ourselves—the view through the enlightening of the divine light (Eph. 1:17; 1 Cor. 2:11-12).

D. We speak what we see with the living words of this life under the inspiration of the Holy Spirit and with His enlightenment (Acts 5:20).

E. For the sake of the building up of the church, we need to build up a habit of speaking the word of the Lord by letting His word dwell in us richly (Col. 3:16; cf. 1 Tim. 6:20).

Morning Nourishment

1 Cor. **But he who prophesies speaks building up and**
14:3 **encouragement and consolation to men.**
   39 **So then, my brothers, desire earnestly the prophe-**
         sying...
3:12 **But if anyone builds upon the foundation gold,**
         silver, precious stones, wood, grass, stubble.

Building up is for the church, encouragement is for the
believers, and consolation is for the saints' spiritual welfare
[1 Cor. 14:3]. Building up, encouragement, and consolation are
not foretelling or predicting. These items indicate that to prophesy is to speak for the Lord and to speak forth the Lord. Some
thoughtful people may wonder how we can interpret 1 Corinthians 14:3 in this way since this verse does not say directly that
to prophesy is to speak for the Lord and to speak forth the Lord.
Instead, it says that he who prophesies speaks to men building
up, encouragement, and consolation. We need to realize, however,
that building up, encouragement, and consolation are Christ
Himself. (*The Advance of the Lord's Recovery Today*, p. 99)

Today's Reading

To speak building up is to speak Christ. Without Christ, how
can we build up the church? To speak building up equals to
speak Christ. Paul is a marvelous writer. He did not say directly
that to prophesy is to speak Christ. If he just said this, people
might understand Christ in a general way as being our Savior
and our Lord. Instead, Paul said that to prophesy is to speak
building up. To speak building up is something deeper. This
building up is the building up of the Body of Christ, which is
the church. With what can we build up the Body of Christ? Can
we build up the Body of Christ with our learning or our ability?
Surely not. We can only build up the Body of Christ with Christ.

Paul tells us in 1 Corinthians 3 that we build up the church
with gold, silver, and precious stones (v. 12). Gold, silver, and
precious stones signify the three main characteristics of the
Triune God, and the embodiment of the Triune God is Christ

(Col. 2:9). Therefore, to speak building up is to speak Christ as the very material with which the church is built up.

First Corinthians 14:3 also says that to prophesy is to speak encouragement. While I am speaking, I may realize that some of the audience is discouraged. Therefore, I have to speak encouragement to them to stir them up. When I speak encouragement to the saints, I speak Christ.

The elders in the church need encouragement every day. Christ is the encouragement to the elders. To be an elder is not an easy thing. Many elders can testify that they receive more discouragement than encouragement. For the church life, for the building up of the Body of Christ, we need encouragement every day. Discouraging matters may come to us, but we should always exercise to call "O Lord Jesus!" Calling on the Lord can bring us out of our discouragement into the heavenlies. In 1 Corinthians 14, Paul refers to Christ hiddenly and mysteriously. To build up the church is the goal of God's economy. For this building up we must experience Christ as our encouragement every day. Christ is not only the material, the constituents, for the building up of the Body of Christ but also the encouragement for the building up of His Body. To prophesy we need to speak Christ as encouragement.

Christ is also consolation. He is the only One who is a consolation to us. Consolation implies more than comfort. To be consoled is to be comforted in the depths of our being. Christ Himself is our consolation. When I speak consolation, I am speaking Christ as consolation. As long as we have building up, encouragement, and consolation, we can build up the Body of Christ. When Paul tells us that to prophesy is to speak building up, encouragement, and consolation, he means that to prophesy is to speak Christ as these items. (*The Advance of the Lord's Recovery Today,* pp. 99, 102-104)

Further Reading: The Advance of the Lord's Recovery Today, ch. 6; *The Excelling Gift for the Building Up of the Church,* ch. 1

Enlightenment and inspiration: _____

_____

_____

_____

Morning Nourishment

1 Cor. So also you, since you are zealous of spirits,
14:12 seek that you may excel for the building up of
the church.

24-25 But if all prophesy and some unbeliever or
unlearned person enters, he is convicted by all,
he is examined by all; the secrets of his heart
become manifest; and so falling on *his* face, he
will worship God, declaring that indeed God is
among you.

Prophesying is excelling in revealing God's heart, God's will,
God's way, and God's economy to His people. When we prophesy, we speak what is on God's heart, and we speak God's will,
God's way, and God's economy. Actually, all the Epistles written by the apostles are books of prophecy, not in the sense of
prediction, but in the sense of speaking for God and speaking
forth God into people. There are some predictions in the Epistles, but mainly they speak for Christ, speak forth Christ, and
speak Christ into people, dispense Christ into people.

If we know how to read the Bible and understand the Bible,
our impression from reading Revelation will not be of predictions, but of a dear One and a near One, who is so lovable and
intimate to us. If we know the New Testament, whatever book
or page we read, we will be impressed with the present Christ,
the Christ today, the Christ this hour. Paul prophesied by
writing his fourteen Epistles. Peter prophesied by writing his
two Epistles. James, John, and Jude did the same by writing
their Epistles. All the Epistles are prophesyings. In the Epistles,
we can see God's heart, God's will, God's way, and God's economy.
(*The Advance of the Lord's Recovery Today*, pp. 111-112)

Today's Reading

Prophesying is also excelling in convicting people, exposing
people's real condition, and showing people their spiritual need.
When people read the twenty-two Epistles of the New Testament,...they are convicted, judged, and all the secrets of their

hearts are exposed, especially the evil secrets. Such speaking shows people their real need, not in material things but in spiritual things. This is why we encourage people to read the New Testament. The four Gospels plus the book of Acts may be considered as historical books. The twenty-two Epistles that follow these books are all prophesying. Each Epistle exposes our condition and shows us our real spiritual need in Christ.

Prophesying is excelling in speaking forth Christ to minister and dispense Christ to people for their nourishment. To prophesy is to dispense Christ into people just as a waiter or a waitress in a restaurant dispenses food to people. When we prophesy, we are dispensing Christ as food to others. What people receive from our prophesying is not a prediction but food for their nourishment.

Prophesying is excelling in building up the church in the organic way that it may be built up as the organism of the processed Triune God for His fullness, His expression. The four factors which we have pointed out above show that prophesying is the excelling gift for the building up of the church, making its seekers excelling.

I have no doubt that the Lord is going to recover the practice of 1 Corinthians 14. Eventually, what the Lord spoke in 1 Corinthians 14 will be fulfilled. The fellowship printed in this book will exist for years to come. If what I am speaking here is not fulfilled in this century, it may be fulfilled in the next century. To the Lord one thousand years are just one day (2 Pet. 3:8). What I have spoken in this book will remain on this globe. Many of the saints will fellowship about this, will be brought into this, and will practice this because it is in the holy Word. Besides God Himself, nothing in this universe is more valuable than the holy Word. First Corinthians 14 is a particular chapter in the holy Word. Paul stressed the matter of all prophesying in this chapter, and he told us we need to pursue, desire, seek, excel, and learn to prophesy. We all have to receive the heavenly enlightenment. (*The Advance of the Lord's Recovery Today,* pp. 112-114)

Further Reading: The Advance of the Lord's Recovery Today, ch. 6

Enlightenment and inspiration: _____
_____
_____
_____

Morning Nourishment

1 Cor. For you can all prophesy one by one that all may
14:31 learn and all may be encouraged.

Rom. I am debtor both to Greeks and to barbarians, both
1:14-15 to wise and to foolish; so, for my part, I am ready to
announce the gospel to you also who are in Rome.

All the believers have the capacity to prophesy and have the
obligation to prophesy (1 Cor. 14:31, 24). The capacity is the
ability. First Corinthians 14:31 says that we can all prophesy
one by one. The word *can* indicates the capacity, the ability, to
prophesy. Any kind of life has a certain capacity. The peach tree
has its life, and in this life there is the capacity to produce
peaches. In our human life, there are many capacities....These
capacities need growth, development, and practice. A little
infant learns to walk through growth, development, and practice. His capacity to walk is developed based on the growth in
life with the help of some instruction from his parents. By
practicing, he is gradually able to progress from crawling to
standing to walking. Eventually, he is able to run and jump.
This is an example of the capacities in our human life.

There are also capacities in the divine life that we have
received. Through regeneration we received another life, the
divine life, which is the eternal life. The divine life is eternal in
space, in time, and in quality. It is altogether unlimited. This
life is full of capacities, and the most striking capacity is the
capacity to speak for God, to prophesy. (*The Advance of the
Lord's Recovery Today,* pp. 115-116)

Today's Reading

The capacity to prophesy is in the divine life, which the
believers possess and enjoy and which needs to increase within
them that the capacity may be developed unto their ability....
Right after someone receives the Lord Jesus and is regenerated,
a desire is put within him to speak something for Christ. He
may not know how to speak, but this desire is within him. As
he begins to speak in the meetings of the church, his speaking

function develops. As he continues to practice speaking, he is like a babe who learns to stand, to walk, and eventually to run and jump. His spiritual function is developed through his practice.

The obligation to prophesy is the fulfillment of our spiritual service, in which we are indebted to God's salvation. Verse 24 says that if all prophesy the unbelievers and unlearned persons are convicted and examined. Verse 31 says that we can all prophesy one by one. These verses show that we all should bear the responsibility to prophesy. We all have the obligation to prophesy. It is so good that we have the capacity to prophesy. This should encourage us. But we also have to realize that we have the obligation to prophesy. We owe something to God and to His dynamic salvation. His salvation is with, by, and in the divine life. In this dynamic salvation, there is the capacity to prophesy. Furthermore, since we are enjoying such a salvation, we are indebted to this salvation. It is our duty to prophesy for the building up of the church. We have received the dynamic salvation, yet we have been annulled by the traditional practice that made us passive. We have to drop the way of the clergy-laity system and come back to the way of every member functioning for the building up of the Body of Christ.

Many of the saints have never prophesied according to the revelation of 1 Corinthians 14. When any of us speaks in a meeting, that meeting becomes the top meeting to us. A certain meeting may be high, but if we do not speak in that meeting, we do not appreciate it that much. A high meeting may be poor in our sight because we did not speak. Even if a meeting was low, if we spoke in that meeting, it became the best meeting to us. To us it was the best meeting because we spoke something. If all of us come together as "pew members," that meeting will be full of death. But if all of us come together, and all of us exercise to speak one by one, that meeting will be in the heavens. It will be the highest meeting. (*The Advance of the Lord's Recovery Today,* pp. 116, 118-119)

Further Reading: The Advance of the Lord's Recovery Today, ch. 7

Enlightenment and inspiration: _____

_____

_____

_____

Morning Nourishment

1 Cor. 14:1 Pursue love, and desire earnestly spiritual *gifts*, but especially that you may prophesy.

12 So also you, since you are zealous of spirits, seek that you may excel for the building up of the church.

31 For you can all prophesy one by one that all may learn and all may be encouraged.

39 So then, my brothers, desire earnestly the prophesying...

All the believers have been charged by the apostle to pursue, to desire earnestly, and to seek to prophesy (1 Cor. 14:1, 12, 39). In verse 1 is the word *pursue*. In verse 12 is the word *seek*. In verse 39 the words *desire earnestly* are used.

We can pursue, desire earnestly, and seek to prophesy by learning (v. 31) in the Word of God, in the growth of life, and in our contact with God. First Corinthians 14:31 says that we can all prophesy one by one that all may learn. When we prophesy, others learn. This proves that before we prophesy, we have learned something. We are enabled to prophesy by learning.

At this point I would like to say a word of love to all of us. We have been chosen by God. We have been called by Him. We have been regenerated by Him and have become sons of God. We must spend sufficient time in the holy Word. We have to do it. We should not say that we do not have any time for this. As long as we have time to eat, we should have time to study the Word of God. Some saints had a proverb that said—"No Bible, no breakfast." This proverb should always be in front of us. Perhaps we should even put it on our desk or hang it on our wall where we can see it every day—"No Bible, no breakfast." (*The Advance of the Lord's Recovery Today*, p. 120)

Today's Reading

If we desire to prophesy, we must learn the holy Word in the Bible. We must get ourselves fully acquainted with all the terms in the Bible. We need to be soaked in the holy Word so that we can be knowledgeable of the holy Word. In Luke 1 there is a record of the Lord's mother, Mary, visiting Elizabeth. Both of them prophesied to one another. Nearly every clause and every phrase of Mary's prophecy was a quotation from the Old Testament. This proves that Mary as a young woman was very knowledgeable of God's Word. We all have to learn the holy Word. If we do not have the holy Word, we do not have the expressions with which to speak. We may have the feeling and the inspiration within, but we will not have the utterances and the wording. All of us have to endeavor to learn the Word.

We also learn to prophesy in the growth of life. A person who has only been saved two months should not expect that he will be able to speak that much. In order to do things properly even in our human life, we have to grow. In the spiritual life it is the same. Spiritually speaking, we pass through stages of infancy, babyhood, childhood, teenage, and then we become a full-grown man. How much we can prophesy depends upon the degree of our growth in life. This is why we must seek the growth in the spiritual life.

We also learn to prophesy in our contact with God. We have to contact God, to fellowship with God. If we get into the Lord's Word, pursue the growth in life, and keep ourselves in contact with God, we will learn to prophesy.

We are also enabled to prophesy by being perfected by the prophets (Eph. 4:12). There are some among us who can do the prophesying work. We should receive the perfecting from these ones. The gifted prophets among us should contact some of the dear saints. Then these saints can be perfected to prophesy.

The saints need to be perfected and instructed, and they must put their instruction into practice. They need to practice by speaking in all the meetings. They should also tell people about Christ to practice prophesying. (*The Advance of the Lord's Recovery Today,* pp. 120-121)

Further Reading: The Advance of the Lord's Recovery Today, ch. 7;
The Excelling Gift for the Building Up of the Church, ch. 2

Enlightenment and inspiration: _____
_____
_____
_____

Morning Nourishment

1 Cor. **What then, brothers? Whenever you come to-**
14:26 **gether, each one has a psalm, has a teaching, has**
a revelation, has a tongue, has an interpretation.
Let all things be done for building up.

Heb. **And let us consider one another so as to incite** *one*
10:24-25 *another* **to love and good works, not abandoning**
our own assembling together, as the custom with
some is, but exhorting *one another;* **and so much**
the more as you see the day drawing near.

In 1937 in Shanghai, Brother Nee spoke to us the messages
which are now in *The Normal Christian Church Life.* In that
fellowship Brother Nee pointed out the way to meet according to
1 Corinthians 14:26. This verse says that when the whole church
comes together, each one has something. The word *has* is used
five times in this verse—"each one has a psalm, has a teaching,
has a revelation, has a tongue, has an interpretation." When
speaking of this verse, Brother Nee used the word *mutuality.* A
church meeting is not a meeting where only one speaks and the
others listen. This is only one-way traffic without mutuality. The
church meeting described in 1 Corinthians 14:26 is full of mutuality. It is a meeting in which all the saints participate by speaking
and listening to one another. Even though Brother Nee saw
this, we did not find a way to carry it out. (*The Excelling Gift
for the Building Up of the Church as the Body of Christ,* p. 23)

Today's Reading

To meet according to 1 Corinthians 14:26, we must desire and
learn to prophesy. Prophesying is so that others may learn; hence,
to prophesy requires learning. If we say something for others
to learn, we have to learn first. We learn to prophesy through
experiences. We have to love the Lord, live Him, and enjoy Him.
We also learn to prophesy by being equipped with the Word
(2 Tim. 3:16-17). We must get into the Word and become saturated
with the Word until we are one with the Word. To learn to
prophesy we need to pray unceasingly (1 Thes. 5:17-20). We need

to pray ourselves into the Spirit. This kind of unceasing prayer will keep us in the Spirit all the time. We must be in the Spirit; otherwise, we cannot have God's oracle. We must be in the Spirit; otherwise, we cannot speak something divine. We learn to prophesy by living and walking by the Spirit (Gal. 5:16, 25). We also learn to prophesy by practicing. Our learning to prophesy is for attending the meeting of mutuality to fulfill 1 Corinthians 14:26.

In Taipei we gave the saints some practical fellowship concerning how to prepare to prophesy in the church meetings on the Lord's Day. Every week they will cover a chapter of a certain book of the Bible and divide this chapter into six portions for six days. In each section for each day, they choose two or three verses for pray-reading, and they enjoy the Lord with these verses for their morning revival. We charged the saints to write down a short reminder of what the Lord inspired them with in their time with Him in the morning. At the end of the week, they will have six notes of what they were inspired with during the week....They use these notes...to compose a prophecy to speak for three minutes. Then they practice it in their homes. They are instructed not to be too long or too short. When they go to the church meeting on the Lord's Day, they have something, thus fulfilling the Lord's word in 1 Corinthians 14:26—"each one has." They do not trust merely in instant inspiration, but they come to the meeting prepared with the riches of Christ that they have enjoyed....The saints need to be perfected to enjoy the Lord, to be saturated with the Word, to pray unceasingly, to fellowship with the Lord moment by moment, to walk in the Spirit, and to speak the Lord in the Spirit at all times. Then they need to learn how to compose a prophecy for the church meetings. I hope that we all would try to practice this for our church meetings. (*The Excelling Gift for the Building Up of the Church,* pp. 30-32)

Further Reading: Life-study of 1 Corinthians, msg. 64; *Prophesying in the Church Meetings for the Organic Building Up of the Church as the Body of Christ (Outlines),* otl. 2

Enlightenment and inspiration: _____

_____
_____
_____

Morning Nourishment

Col. Let the word of Christ dwell in you richly in all
3:16 wisdom, teaching and admonishing one another
with psalms *and* hymns *and* spiritual songs, singing with grace in your hearts to God.

Acts Go and stand in the temple and speak to the people
5:20 all the words of this life.

1 Cor. And the spirits of prophets are subject to prophets.
14:32

According to our study of the New Testament, there are
three constituting elements of prophesying: God's living word
of life (Acts 5:20), the instant moving of the Spirit, and the view
through the enlightening of the divine light. First, we need to
be acquainted with the living word, so we need to read the Bible
every day. Every morning we should spend ten minutes to
pray-read two verses, dwell upon them, and enjoy the Lord in
them. If we drive to work, we can pray-read these verses again
on the way. If we pray-read two verses a day for six days a week,
we can be saturated with six hundred twenty-four verses in a
year. We will become saturated, soaked, and fully acquainted
with these verses. This will give us the knowledge of the Word,
and the proper expressions and utterance in our speaking.

The second element we need is the instant inspiration of the
Spirit. Because we are persons dwelling in the Word, we will be in
the fellowship of the Lord, and our spirit will be exercised and ready
to receive the instant inspiration of the Holy Spirit at any time.

Third, we need the view through the enlightening of the
divine light. Our sky needs to be clear. Under the divine
enlightenment we can see the real situation of ourselves, the
church, and the saints. Because we have such a view, we can
speak when the inspiration comes. We speak what we see with
the divine word under the inspiration of the Spirit and with His
enlightenment. This is prophesying. (*The Practical and Organic Building Up of the Church*, pp. 44-45)

Today's Reading

First, in order to prophesy we must be persons who have been saturated and soaked with the holy Word....Second, in order to learn to prophesy, we must be ready in the spirit to have the inspiration of the Holy Spirit (1 Cor. 14:32). A ready spirit is a spirit that is always one with the Lord, the Spirit, fellowshipping with Him, remaining with Him, and abiding in Him. When we have such a ready spirit, we can have the spiritual inspiration at any time. We can even tell the Lord: "Please give me the inspiration. I am ready in my spirit, and I have to prophesy." To prophesy, we need the knowledge of the Word and the inspiration of the Holy Spirit. The knowledge of the Word is constant, and the inspiration of the Holy Spirit is instant. The instant inspiration depends upon our constant readiness. We have to be constantly ready in our spirit to receive the instant inspiration of the Holy Spirit.

If we only have the knowledge of the Word and the inspiration of the Holy Spirit, we still will not be able to prophesy. We need to have a clear view to see through all things in all situations. We will not know what to say without a vision. We need to have a clear sky all the time. We need to be sober in our mind and in our spirit. We need a clear view concerning the Lord's interest on this earth, concerning His Body, concerning the local churches, concerning the individual saints, and even concerning ourselves.

If we have the three items mentioned above, we can prophesy at any time. With a clear view to see, we have something to speak. We also have the ability to speak because we have the knowledge of the Word for the utterance and the proper expressions. Furthermore, we have the inspiration of the Holy Spirit. When we speak with these three elements, our speaking is the speaking of the Lord and the speaking forth of the Lord. (*The Present Advance of the Lord's Recovery,* pp. 59-60)

Further Reading: The Practical and Organic Building Up of the Church, ch. 4; The Present Advance of the Lord's Recovery, ch. 4; Prophesying in the Church Meetings for the Organic Building Up of the Church as the Body of Christ (Outlines), otl. 6

Enlightenment and inspiration: _____

_____

_____

_____

Hymns, #864

1   Whene'er we meet with Christ endued,
     The surplus of His plenitude
  We offer unto God as food,
     And thus exhibit Christ.

     Let us exhibit Christ,
     Let us exhibit Christ;
  We'll bring His surplus to the church
     And thus exhibit Christ.

2   In Christ we live, by Christ we fight,
     On Christ we labor day and night,
  And with His surplus we unite
     To thus exhibit Christ.

3   Our life and all we are and do
     Is Christ Himself, the substance true,
  That every time we meet anew
     We may exhibit Christ.

4   In meetings Christ to God we bear
     And Christ with one another share,
  And Christ with God enjoying there,
     We thus exhibit Christ.

5   The risen Christ to God we bring,
     And Christ ascended offering,
  God's satisfaction answering,
     We thus exhibit Christ.

6   The center and reality,
     The atmosphere and ministry,
  Of all our meetings is that we
     May thus exhibit Christ.

7   The testimony and the prayer,
     And all the fellowship we share,
  The exercise of gifts, whate'er,
     Should just exhibit Christ.

8   The Father we would glorify,
     Exalting Christ the Son, thereby
  The meeting's purpose satisfy
     That we exhibit Christ.

Composition for prophecy with main point and sub-points: _____

_____

_____

_____

_____

_____

_____

_____

_____

_____

_____

_____

_____

_____

_____

_____

_____

_____

_____

_____

_____

_____

_____

_____

_____

_____

_____

_____

_____

_____

_____

_____

_____

_____

_____

_____

Christ Becoming the Life-giving Spirit through Resurrection

Scripture Reading: 1 Cor. 15:45b, 10, 58; Phil. 1:19; Exo. 30:23-25

Day 1 I. **In 1 Corinthians 15, Paul dealt with the Corinthians' heretical saying that there is no resurrection of the dead; we must see that resurrection is the life pulse and lifeline of the divine economy (v. 12):**

A. The three major items of the Lord's resurrection are the birth of the firstborn Son of God, the regeneration of the many sons of God, and Christ as the last Adam becoming a life-giving Spirit; the entire economy of God is carried out by these three items (Acts 13:33; 1 Pet. 1:3; 1 Cor. 15:45b):

1. The firstborn Son of God is the Head of the Body (Col. 1:18), the many sons of God are the members of the Body (John 12:24; Rom. 8:29), and the life-giving Spirit is the reality and life of the Body (John 14:17; Eph. 4:4).

2. Without these major items of the Lord's resurrection, there would be no church, no Body of Christ, and there would be no economy of God.

Day 2 B. If there were no resurrection, God would be the God of the dead, not of the living (Matt. 22:32).

C. If there were no resurrection, Christ would not have been raised from the dead; He would be a dead Savior, not a living One who lives forever (Rev. 1:18) and is able to save to the uttermost (Heb. 7:25).

D. If there were no resurrection, there would be no living proof of our being justified by His death (Rom. 4:25), no imparting of life (John 12:24), no regeneration (3:5), no renewing (Titus 3:5), no

transformation (Rom. 12:2; 2 Cor. 3:18), and no
conformity to the image of Christ (Rom. 8:29).

E. If there were no resurrection, there would be no
members of Christ (12:5), no Body of Christ as
His fullness (Eph. 1:20-23), and no church as
Christ's bride (John 3:29), and therefore no new
man (Eph. 2:15; 4:24; Col. 3:10-11).

F. If there were no resurrection, God's New Testament economy would altogether collapse and
God's eternal purpose would be nullified.

Day 3 **II. In incarnation Christ became flesh for redemption (John 1:14, 29); then in resurrection
He became a life-giving Spirit for the impar-
tation of life to make us men of life (10:10b;
1 Cor. 15:45b; Rom. 8:10, 6, 11):**

A. Through and in His resurrection, Christ as the
last Adam became the life-giving Spirit to enter
into His believers to flow out as rivers of living
water (John 7:37-39; Rev. 21:6; 22:17).

B. The life-giving Spirit is the Spirit of Jesus
Christ, comprising all the elements of Jesus'
humanity with His death and Christ's divinity
with His resurrection, which become the bountiful supply of the unsearchable Christ for the
support of His believers (Phil. 1:19b).

Day 4 C. The life-giving Spirit is a compound Spirit, typified by the compound anointing ointment with
its ingredients (Exo. 30:23-25; 1 John 2:20, 27):

1. Olive oil signifies the Spirit of God with
divinity:

a. Olive oil is the base of the compound ointment, the holy anointing oil (Isa. 61:1-2;
Heb. 1:9).

b. Olive oil, produced by the pressing of
olives (cf. Matt. 26:36), is for the priest-
hood and the kingship to proclaim the
jubilee of grace (Lev. 8:12; 1 Sam. 16:12-
13; Luke 4:18-19).

2. Myrrh signifies the precious death of Christ:

   a. Myrrh was used to reduce pain and heal the body when it gave off the wrong kind of secretion (Mark 15:23; John 19:39).

   b. The Spirit was compounded through Christ's sufferings in His living a cruci-fied life, a life of myrrh, from the manger to the cross as the first God-man (Matt. 2:11; John 19:39; Isa. 53:2-3).

   c. The Spirit leads us to the cross, the cross is applied by the Spirit, and the cross issues in more abundance of the Spirit (Heb. 9:14; Rom. 6:3, 6; 8:13-14; Gal. 2:20; John 12:24).

Day 5

3. Cinnamon typifies the sweetness and effec-tiveness of Christ's death:

   a. Cinnamon was used to stimulate a weak heart (Neh. 8:10; Isa. 42:4a).

   b. We are conformed to the death of Christ by our outward, consuming environment in cooperation with the indwelling, cru-cifying Spirit (2 Cor. 4:10-11, 16; Rom. 8:13-14; Gal. 5:24; Col. 3:5; Gal. 6:17).

4. Calamus signifies the precious resurrec-tion of Christ:

   a. Calamus is a reed standing up (shooting into the air) and growing in a marsh or muddy place (1 Pet. 3:18).

   b. We need to experience the Spirit as the reality of Christ's resurrection (John 11:25; 20:22; Lam. 3:55-57).

5. Cassia signifies the repelling power of Christ's resurrection:

   a. Cinnamon is from the inner part of the bark, and cassia, from the outer part (Rev. 2:7; 1 Pet. 2:24; John 11:25).

   b. Cassia was a repellent to drive away insects and snakes (Eph. 6:11, 17b-18).

c. We need to know the power of Christ's resurrection in the life-giving Spirit as the all-sufficient grace of the processed and consummated Triune God (Phil. 3:10; 2 Cor. 12:9-10; 1 Cor. 15:10, 45b, 58; Phil. 4:23).

Day 6   D. The life-giving Spirit is the Lord Spirit, the pneumatic Christ, for the metabolic transformation of the believers and for the growth and building up of the Body of Christ (2 Cor. 3:17-18; 1 Cor. 3:6, 9b, 12a; Eph. 4:16b).

E. Without Christ being the life-giving Spirit, we cannot experience anything of God in His economy (1 John 5:6; John 16:13; 1 Cor. 15:45b; 2:10; 6:17).

III. **Grace is the resurrected Christ becoming the life-giving Spirit to bring the processed Triune God in resurrection into us to be our life and life supply that we may live in resurrection (15:10, 45b):**

A. The grace that motivated the apostle and operated in him was a living person, the resurrected Christ as the life-giving Spirit (John 1:17; Gal. 2:20-21; cf. 1 Cor. 15:10).

B. His ministry and living by this grace were an undeniable testimony to Christ's resurrection (vv. 8-10, 31, 58).

Morning Nourishment

Acts   That God has fully fulfilled this *promise* to us their
13:33 children in raising up Jesus, as it is also written
       in the second Psalm, "You are My Son; this day
       have I begotten You."

1 Pet. Blessed be the God and Father of our Lord Jesus
   1:3 Christ, who according to His great mercy has
        regenerated us unto a living hope through the
        resurrection of Jesus Christ from the dead.

1 Cor. ...The last Adam *became* a life-giving Spirit.
15:45

In the raising up of Christ, in this divine act, God accomplished
three big things. He produced the firstborn Son, the many sons,
and the life-giving Spirit. The entire economy of God is carried
out by these three items. If you were to delete Acts 13:33, 1 Peter
1:3, and 1 Corinthians 15:45b from the Bible, the firstborn Son
of God, the many sons of God, and the life-giving Spirit would
be absent from the divine revelation. Even though these items
concerning the resurrection of Christ are in the Bible, they are
mostly absent from the fundamental teaching of today's Christianity. Without these major items of the Lord's resurrection, there
would be no church, no Body of Christ. If there were nothing in
the Bible revealing the firstborn Son of God, the many sons of
God, and the life-giving Spirit, there would be no economy of God.
These items are new to many Christians, but they are not new
to the Bible. (*The Practical Way to Live a Life according to the
High Peak of the Divine Revelation in the Holy Scriptures*, p. 35)

Today's Reading

Resurrection implies three big things. First, in resurrection,
Christ was born to be the firstborn Son of God....Who has ever
thought that besides the incarnation, Christ had another birth
in His resurrection?

This day in [Acts 13:33] was the day of resurrection. Christ
was begotten by God in resurrection to be God's firstborn Son.
...Christ was the only begotten Son of God even before His
incarnation (John 1:18). His incarnation was the coming of the only

begotten Son of God (3:16). This Son of God was incarnated to be a man. But Acts 13:33 unveils that in resurrection God begot Christ to be the firstborn Son of God among many brothers (Rom. 8:29).

Also, the Bible tells us that we, the God-chosen people, were regenerated in Christ's resurrection [1 Pet. 1:3]....God has regenerated us through the resurrection of Christ. In resurrection God begot a Son, Jesus Christ, and in resurrection God regenerated many sons. This shows us that the resurrection of Christ was a great delivery. In that same delivery, the Firstborn was Christ, and this firstborn Brother had many "twins" to follow Him. In the unique resurrection Christ was born and we were regenerated, so we were His "twins" in the same delivery.

Now we come to the third great thing accomplished in Christ's resurrection. We have seen that in the same resurrection, Christ was born to be the firstborn Son of God, and we the God-chosen people were born to be the many sons of God, who are the "twins" of Christ. Also, in this same resurrection, Christ became a life-giving Spirit. The holy Scriptures say in 1 Corinthians 15:45b, "The last Adam became a life-giving Spirit."

There are three marvelous verses which show us the intrinsic significance of Christ's resurrection. First, Acts 13:33 tells us that in resurrection God accomplished a birth. In resurrection God begot Christ to be His firstborn Son. Then 1 Peter 1:3 tells us that through resurrection God regenerated us, the millions of God-chosen people. There was such a great delivery, a great begetting, in resurrection. Third, 1 Corinthians 15:45b tells us that in resurrection the last Adam, the man Jesus, became a life-giving Spirit. These three great things took place and were accomplished in the resurrection of Christ. (*The Practical Way to Live a Life according to the High Peak of the Divine Revelation in the Holy Scriptures,* pp. 33-34)

Further Reading: The Practical Way to Live a Life according to the High Peak of the Divine Revelation in the Holy Scriptures, chs. 3-4; *Life-study of 1 Corinthians,* msgs. 65-66

Enlightenment and inspiration: _____

_____

_____

_____

Morning Nourishment

Matt. "I am the God of Abraham and the God of Isaac
22:32 and the God of Jacob"? He is not the God of the
dead, but of the living.

Heb. Hence also He is able to save to the uttermost
7:25 those who come forward to God through Him,
since He lives always to intercede for them.

Rom. Who was delivered for our offenses and was raised
4:25 for our justification.

John Truly, truly, I say to you, Unless the grain of wheat
12:24 falls into the ground and dies, it abides alone; but
if it dies, it bears much fruit.

In 1 Corinthians 15 the apostle deals with the Corinthians'
heretical saying that there is no resurrection of the dead. They
were like the Sadducees (Matt. 22:23; Acts 23:8). This is the
tenth problem among them. It is the most damaging and
destructive to God's New Testament economy, worse than the
heresy of Hymenaeus and Philetus concerning resurrection in
2 Timothy 2:17 and 18. Resurrection is the life pulse and lifeline
of the divine economy. If there were no resurrection, God would
be the God of the dead, not the God of the living (Matt. 22:32).
If there were no resurrection, Christ would not have been raised
from the dead. He would be a dead Savior, not the One who
lives forever (Rev. 1:18) and is able to save to the uttermost
(Heb. 7:25). If there is no resurrection, there would be no living
proof of justification by His death (Rom. 4:25), no imparting of
life (John 12:24), no regeneration (John 3:5), no renewing (Titus
3:5), no transformation (Rom. 12:2; 2 Cor. 3:18), and no conformity to the image of Christ (Rom. 8:29). If there were no
resurrection, there would be no members of Christ (Rom. 12:5),
no Body of Christ as His fullness (Eph. 1:20-23), and no church
as Christ's bride (John 3:29) and the new man (Eph. 2:15; 4:24;
Col. 3:10-11). If there were no resurrection, God's New Testament economy would altogether collapse and God's eternal
purpose would be nullified. (*Life-study of 1 Corinthians*,
pp. 593-594)

Today's Reading

In my heart I have a burden to tell you the intrinsic contents of the New Testament....The New Testament presents to us four acts of God and three products of these four acts. These three products issue in one ultimate goal and consummation. The four acts of God are His incarnation, human living, death, and resurrection. The three products are the firstborn Son of God, the many sons of God, and the life-giving Spirit. The unique, ultimate consummation is the New Jerusalem. We need to see these four acts, three products, and one goal.

The act of God in resurrection produced three great items. Before the resurrection, there was no firstborn Son of God (Acts 13:33). He was produced in God's action in resurrection. Also, before the resurrection, there were no men becoming sons of God in this universe. But we were all produced as the sons of God in His act in resurrection (1 Pet. 1:3). John 7:39 says that "the Spirit was not yet" before Jesus was glorified in His resurrection. First Corinthians 15:45b reveals that in resurrection, the last Adam, Christ, became a life-giving Spirit.

This life-giving Spirit is "the Spirit" in John 7:39. The life-giving Spirit, even at the Lord Jesus' time on earth, was still "not yet." Then Christ became the life-giving Spirit in resurrection, and this life-giving Spirit is the consummation of the processed and consummated Triune God....The last Adam became the life-giving Spirit....So the embodiment of the Triune God became the life-giving Spirit. Therefore, the life-giving Spirit is the consummation of the processed and consummated Triune God. (*The Practical Way to Live a Life according to the High Peak of the Divine Revelation in the Holy Scriptures,* pp. 42-43)

Further Reading: Life-study of 1 Corinthians, msgs. 65-66; The Practical Way to Live a Life according to the High Peak of the Divine Revelation in the Holy Scriptures, chs. 3-4

Enlightenment and inspiration: _____
_____
_____
_____

Morning Nourishment

John 7:37-39 Now on the last day, the great *day* of the feast, Jesus stood and cried out, saying, If anyone thirsts, let him come to Me and drink. He who believes into Me, as the Scripture said, out of his innermost being shall flow rivers of living water. But this He said concerning the Spirit, whom those who believed into Him were about to receive; for *the* Spirit was not yet, because Jesus had not yet been glorified.

1 Cor. 15:45 ...The last Adam *became* a life-giving Spirit.

First Corinthians 15:45 says, "So also it is written, 'The first man, Adam, became a living soul'; the last Adam became a life-giving Spirit." Adam became a living soul through creation with a soulish body. Christ became a life-giving Spirit through resurrection with a spiritual body. Adam as a living soul is natural; Christ as a life-giving Spirit is resurrected. First, in incarnation, He became flesh for redemption (John 1:14, 29). Then in resurrection He became a life-giving Spirit for imparting life (John 10:10). He had a soulish body like Adam through incarnation. He has a spiritual body through resurrection. His soulish body has become a spiritual one through resurrection. Now He is a life-giving Spirit in resurrection, with a spiritual body, ready to be received by His believers. When we believe into Him, He enters our spirit, and we are joined to Him as the life-giving Spirit. Hence, we become one spirit with Him (1 Cor. 6:17). Our spirit is made alive and resurrected with Him. Eventually our present soulish body will also become a spiritual body in resurrection just as His body is (1 Cor. 15:52-54; Phil. 3:21). (*Life-study of 1 Corinthians,* p. 613)

Today's Reading

Through and in His resurrection Christ as the last Adam became the life-giving Spirit to enter into His believers to flow out as rivers of living water (1 Cor. 15:45b; Rev. 21:6; 22:17c). God is a Spirit and the second of the Triune God in the flesh became a life-giving Spirit. Prior to Christ's resurrection, God was a Spirit but not a life-giving Spirit. Before Christ's death and resurrection, God had no way to enter into man to be man's life. Between man and God there were a number of negative things as obstacles....A fallen, sinful, unclean man was altogether unable to take the tree of life, to take God in as life, until Christ's death fulfilled these requirements.

Hebrews 10 reveals that the death of Christ opened the way, a new and living way, so that we can go into the Holy of Holies to partake of God as the tree of life (vv. 19-20). In His death He fulfilled all the requirements of God's glory, holiness, and righteousness; then in resurrection He changed in form to be the life-giving Spirit. This was absolutely for the organic union between God and man—to bring God into man and to bring man into God in His resurrection. Today we can take the tree of life and drink the water of life so that the Triune God can flow out from our innermost being as rivers of living water.

We have seen that John 7:39 says, "The Spirit was not yet."...The Spirit of God was there from the beginning, but at the time the Lord spoke this word, the Spirit as the Spirit of Christ (Rom. 8:9), the Spirit of Jesus Christ (Phil. 1:19), was not yet, because the Lord had not yet been glorified.

For Jesus to be glorified was for Him to be resurrected (Luke 24:26). Before Christ was resurrected, the Spirit who would flow into the believers and flow out of them as rivers of living water was not yet. His being glorified may be likened to the blossoming of a flower. When the flower blossoms, that is its glorification. Jesus was glorified in resurrection. The Spirit flowing into and out of the believers...would not come into being until after Jesus' resurrection. It was through the resurrection and after the resurrection of Jesus, that the Spirit became the life-giving Spirit (1 Cor. 15:45b) to enter into the believers and flow out of them as rivers of living water. (*The Spirit with Our Spirit,* pp. 25-26, 29)

Further Reading: Life-study of 1 Corinthians, msg. 68; *The Spirit with Our Spirit,* chs. 2-3*

Enlightenment and inspiration: _____

_____

_____

_____

Morning Nourishment

Exo.   You also take the finest spices: of flowing myrrh
30:23-25   five hundred *shekels*, and of fragrant cinnamon
         half as much, two hundred fifty *shekels*, and of
         fragrant calamus two hundred fifty *shekels*, and
         of cassia five hundred *shekels*, according to the
         shekel of the sanctuary, and a hin of olive oil. And
         you shall make it a holy anointing oil, a perfume
         compounded according to the perfumer's art; it
         shall be a holy anointing oil.

1 John   And you have an anointing from the Holy One, and
2:20   all of you know.

The materials of the holy anointing oil are of two categories
and are five in number. The first category includes four spices:
myrrh, cinnamon, calamus, and cassia. The second category
consists of one item—olive oil.

Flowing myrrh, smelling sweet but tasting bitter, signifies
the precious death of Christ. In the Bible myrrh is used mostly
for burial. Hence, myrrh is related to death. According to
John 19, when Nicodemus and others were preparing to bury
the body of the Lord Jesus, they used myrrh....No doubt, the
myrrh in Exodus 30 is a symbol of the Lord's death.

The aromatic liquid of myrrh...can be used for healing the
body when it gives off the wrong kind of secretion. Myrrh can
correct this condition in the human body. In our human life there
are many wrong secretions, but the Lord's death on the cross
corrects this problem. (*Life-study of Exodus,* pp. 1687-1688)

Today's Reading

Fragrant cinnamon signifies the sweetness and effectiveness of Christ's death. Cinnamon not only has a distinctive
flavor, but it can also be used to stimulate the heart.

Myrrh signifies the precious death of Christ, and cinnamon
signifies the effectiveness of His death. If we apply the Lord's
death to our situation, it will reduce our pain, correct the wrong

secretions, and eventually stimulate us and make us happy and joyful....When I apply the Lord's death, I am corrected, adjusted, stimulated, and stirred up.

The calamus in Exodus 30 is a reed. The Hebrew root of the word *myrrh* means "flowing," and the root for *calamus* means "standing up." Calamus grows in a marsh or muddy place. But... it is able to shoot up into the air. According to the sequence of the spices, this calamus signifies the rising up of the Lord Jesus from the place of death. The Lord was put into a marsh, into a death situation, but in resurrection He rose up and stood up. Calamus, therefore, signifies the precious resurrection of Christ.

The fourth spice, cassia, signifies the power of Christ's resurrection. Cassia and cinnamon belong to the same family....Furthermore, the plants from which they are derived often live and grow in places where other plants cannot grow.

In ancient times cassia was used as a repellent to drive away insects and snakes. Cassia thus signifies the power, the effectiveness, of Christ's resurrection. Christ's resurrection can withstand any kind of environment, and His resurrection...repels all evil "insects" and especially the old serpent, the devil.

Myrrh, cinnamon, calamus, and cassia are all of one category of materials, the category of the spices. Now we come to the olive oil, the only item in the second category.

In the Bible olive oil signifies the Spirit of God. Olive oil is produced by the pressing of olives. The olive oil signifies the Spirit of God, through the pressure of Christ's death, flowing out.

The olive oil is the base of the ointment; it is the basic element compounded with the spices. The four spices are compounded into the olive oil to make the ointment. This indicates that the Spirit of God, signified by the olive oil, is no longer merely oil, but now it is oil compounded with certain ingredients. (*Life-study of Exodus,* pp. 1688-1689)

Further Reading: Life-study of Exodus, msgs. 157-159, 163-164; *The Spirit with Our Spirit,* ch. 4

Enlightenment and inspiration: _____

_____

_____

_____

Morning Nourishment

2 Cor. **Always bearing about in the body the putting to**
4:10   **death of Jesus that the life of Jesus also may be**
      manifested in our body.

16 **Therefore we do not lose heart; but though our**
      outer man is decaying, yet our inner *man* is being
      renewed day by day.

Rom. **For if you live according to the flesh, you must die,**
8:13   **but if by the Spirit you put to death the practices**
      of the body, you will live.

Gal. **But they who are of Christ Jesus have crucified**
5:24   **the flesh with its passions and its lusts.**

The putting to death of Jesus in our environment cooperates with the indwelling Spirit to kill our natural man (our outer man), comprising our body and our soul. This is mentioned emphatically in 2 Corinthians 4:10-12. Paul said that he was bearing about in his body the putting to death of Jesus that the life of Jesus might be manifested in his body.

We have the indwelling Spirit within us, but because we are sometimes stiff-necked and stubborn, God raises up the environment to deal with us. The entire situation of our living rises up against us to help the indwelling Spirit. The indwelling Spirit works to kill us. The Spirit is the Killer, but He needs an instrument, a "knife," to kill us. The "knife" may be a brother's wife, his children, or certain brothers and sisters in the church. A certain saint can become a "knife" which the Spirit uses to kill us. (*The Christian Life*, p. 105)

Today's Reading

We all like to have a nice environment, with everything smooth, peaceful, sweet, and nice. When people ask us, "How are you?" We always say, "Fine." Many times when we say this, however, we are lying. If we were fully honest, we would respond by saying, "Not so good." This is because we are under an environment of sufferings and pressures which works with the Spirit to kill our natural man. Brother Nee referred to this kind of environment as the discipline of the Holy Spirit. The putting to death, the killing, in 2 Corinthians 4 is through the environment. In speaking about the application of Christ's death, Romans 8 refers to the indwelling Spirit, while 2 Corinthians 4 refers to the outward environment. The outward environment cooperates with the inward Spirit to carry out the killing of our natural man.

The word *decaying* [in 2 Corinthians 4:16] means "being consumed," "being wasted away," "being worn out."...As our outer man is being consumed by the killing work of death, our inner man is being renewed with the fresh supply of the resurrection life.

We should cooperate with the operating Spirit and accept the environment in our spirit, soul, and body. In every part of our being, we must be willing to cooperate with the indwelling Spirit and to accept the outward environment. Then we are acting under the killing of Christ. This killing is carried out by the indwelling Spirit with the environment as the killing weapon.

In order to cooperate with the operating Spirit and accept the outward environment, we need to recognize that we have been crucified with Christ (Rom. 6:6; Gal. 2:20a). We also need to crucify our flesh with its passions and its lusts (Gal. 5:24). In one sense, we cannot crucify ourselves. But in another sense, we can crucify our flesh with its passions and lusts because we have the new man. The new man crucifies the flesh. This is why we need to exercise our spirit, the new man, to crucify our flesh, our outer man.

We also need to put to death, by the Spirit, the practices of our body (Rom. 8:13b). To put to death means to kill. We need to kill the practices of our body. Whatever our body of sin does, needs to be killed. To gossip on the telephone is a practice of the body which needs to be killed. (*The Christian Life,* pp. 105-106)

Further Reading: The Christian Life, chs. 8-9; *The Spirit,* ch. 12

Enlightenment and inspiration: _____

_____

_____

_____

Morning Nourishment

1 John   This is He who came through water and blood,
5:6   Jesus Christ; not in the water only, but in the
water and in the blood; and the Spirit is He who
testifies, because the Spirit is the reality.

1 Cor.   But by the grace of God I am what I am; and His
15:10   grace unto me did not turn out to be in vain, but,
on the contrary, I labored more abundantly than
all of them, yet not I but the grace of God which is
with me.

45   ...The last Adam *became* a life-giving Spirit.

Gal.   I am crucified with Christ; and *it is* no longer I *who*
2:20   live, but *it is* Christ *who* lives in me...

We need to realize that without the Spirit, we cannot experience anything of God in His economy. No Spirit, no God the
Father. No Spirit, no God the Son. No Spirit, no God the Spirit.
No Spirit, no uplifted, glorified Man. No Spirit, no death of
Christ. No Spirit, no effectiveness of the death of Christ. Without
the Spirit, the death of Christ is far away from us in time and
space. But with the Spirit, Christ's death is here to kill us, to
crucify our old man. No Spirit, no resurrection. No Spirit, no
salvation. No Spirit, no regeneration. No Spirit, no renewing. No
Spirit, no sanctification. No Spirit, no transformation. No Spirit,
no conformation. No Spirit, no glorification. Every positive
thing in this universe in the economy of God is compounded in
this Spirit. Today we can see, by God's enlightenment, the all-
inclusiveness of the Spirit. (*The Christian Life,* pp. 102-103)

Today's Reading

In 1 Corinthians 15:10 Paul continues....Grace, three times
in this verse, is the resurrected Christ becoming the life-giving
Spirit (v. 45) to bring the processed God in resurrection into us
to be our life and life supply that we may live in resurrection.
Thus, grace is the Triune God becoming life and everything to
us. It is by this grace that Saul of Tarsus, the foremost of sinners

(1 Tim. 1:15-16), became the foremost apostle, laboring more abundantly than all the other apostles. His ministry and living by this grace are an undeniable testimony to Christ's resurrection.

"Not I but the grace of God" equals "no longer I...but... Christ" in Galatians 2:20. The grace that motivates the apostle and operates in him is not some matter or some thing, but a living person, the resurrected Christ, the embodiment of God the Father becoming the all-inclusive life-giving Spirit, who dwells in him as his everything.

In 1 Corinthians 15:10 grace is the Christ who is in resurrection and who is resurrection. By this grace Paul could be what he was and labor more than all the other apostles. When we compare 1 Corinthians 15:10 with Galatians 2:20, we see that grace is not a thing, but a person. All the disciples and apostles who saw the resurrected Christ not only saw Him objectively, but experienced Him subjectively. Through their seeing of Christ, He entered into them and became the subjective One in them. When the day of Pentecost came, this was the reason they were living, energetic, and operative. The resurrected Christ was in them. Not only was Christ Himself resurrected objectively, but in resurrection He lived in Peter, John, and all the other apostles and disciples.

Throughout the centuries, all the living servants of God have had this resurrected Christ living in them. I can also testify that He lives in me, enabling me to do what I never could do in myself. Hallelujah, the Lord Jesus lives! How do we know He lives? As the hymn says, we know He lives because He lives in us (*Hymns*, #503). We may be persecuted and opposed, and we may suffer very much. But we have the resurrected Christ in us. The more we are opposed, the more alive and active we become. Nevertheless, our testimony is this: "Not I" but the grace of God with us. (*Life-study of 1 Corinthians,* pp. 591-592)

Further Reading: The Spirit with Our Spirit, ch. 3; Life-study of 1 Corinthians, msg. 65

Enlightenment and inspiration: _____

_____

_____

_____

Hymns, #539

1   O Lord, Thou art in me as life
     And everything to me!
   Subjective and available,
     Thus I experience Thee.

     O Lord, Thou art the Spirit!
       How dear and near to me!
     How I admire Thy marvelous
       Availability!

2   To all my needs both great and small
     Thou art the rich supply;
   So ready and sufficient too
     For me now to apply.

3   Thy sweet anointing with Thy might
     In weakness doth sustain;
   By Thy supply of energy
     My strength Thou dost maintain.

4   Thy law of life in heart and mind
     My conduct regulates;
   The wealth of Thy reality
     My being saturates.

5   O Thou art ever one with me,
     Unrivaled unity!
   One spirit with me all the time
     For all eternity!

Composition for prophecy with main point and sub-points: _____

_____

_____

_____

_____

_____

_____

_____

_____

_____

_____

_____

_____

_____

_____

_____

_____

_____

_____

_____

_____

_____

_____

_____

_____

_____

_____

_____

_____

_____

_____

_____

_____

_____

_____

**Being under the Divine Administration
in Resurrection to Overcome Money
and Material Possessions**

Scripture Reading: 1 Cor. 16:1-3; Matt. 6:24

Day 1   I. Although the material things were created by
God and belong to Him (1 Chron. 29:14, 16),
they have been corrupted by man's fall and
usurped by Satan, the evil one (1 John 5:19);
hence, they belong to fallen man and are unrighteous (Luke 16:9):

   A. Man fell into the darkness of acknowledging
   only material riches and not God, of trusting
   only in material riches and not in God, and even
   of serving material riches, taking them as God
   and allowing them to replace God (1 Tim. 6:17).

   B. To us who believe in the Lord Jesus, the earthly
   things which are necessary for human existence
   may simply be earthly things or they may become the world, a system of Satan (1 John 2:15).

Day 2   II. "No one can serve two masters, for either he
will hate the one and love the other, or he will
hold to one and despise the other. You cannot
serve God and mammon" (Matt. 6:24):

   A. *Mammon* is an Aramaic word signifying wealth,
   riches.

   B. Mammon stands in opposition to God, indicating that wealth, or riches, is the opponent of God,
   robbing God's people of their service to Him.

   C. To serve the Lord requires us to love Him, giving
   our heart to Him, and requires us to cleave to
   Him, giving our entire being to Him (Luke 16:13):

      1. In this way we are released from being occu-
      pied and usurped by mammon, that we may
      serve the Lord wholly and fully.

      2. In Luke 16:13 the Lord emphasizes that to serve
      Him we must overcome the enticing, deceitful
      mammon of unrighteousness (v. 9; Matt. 13:22).

Day 3 III. **The dealing with mammon and material possessions is related to God's administration
among the churches in resurrection (1 Cor.
16:1-3):**

A. If we know resurrection life and the resurrection
power, we shall overcome money and material
possessions; they will have no power over us,
and they will not occupy or possess us (Acts
2:44-45; 4:32-35):

1. Money or material possessions will not hin-
der or frustrate our function in the Body.

2. What we have will be used for God's administration among the churches (1 Cor. 16:1, 3;
Rom. 15:26).

3. If this is our situation, the Lord God will
have a way to carry out His administration
among us.

Day 4 B. Paul opens 1 Corinthians 16 with a word about
collecting material gifts on the first day of the
week (vv. 1-2):

1. The first day of the week signifies resurrection, for it is the day of resurrection (John
20:1; Rev. 1:10).

2. The fact that material things are offered on
the first day of the week indicates that they
should be offered in resurrection, not in our
natural life (Matt. 6:1-4).

3. Giving money and material things in resurrection is a strong indication that we are under
God's administration in resurrection and have
overcome the possession of material riches.

Day 5 IV. **All the material riches and enjoyment in our
living are supplied by God's rich giving;
hence, we must not set our hope on the uncertainty of deceitful riches but on God, who
affords us all things richly for our enjoyment
(1 Tim. 6:17-19; Matt. 13:22).**

V. **The Lord Jesus charges us to store up treasures in heaven, that is, to spend our riches on**

the heavenly Father by doing things such as giving to the poor (Matt. 19:21) and caring for the needy saints (Acts 2:45; 4:34-35; 11:29; Rom. 15:26) and the Lord's servants (Phil. 4:16-17) (Matt. 6:19-21).

VI. To make friends by means of the mammon of unrighteousness is to use money to do things to help others according to God's leading (Luke 16:9).

VII. If we are willing to distribute our material wealth to help the needy for the sake of God, He will give into our bosom that which is rich and plenteous, a good measure, pressed down, shaken together, and running over; He will not give into our hands that which is scanty (6:38).

VIII. The best way to be blessed by God in material riches is to give, not to receive, just as the Lord Jesus did (Acts 20:35; 2 Cor. 8:9).

IX. Supplying the saints with material riches is a fellowship which brings mutual grace to both the giver and the receiver (v. 4).

X. Offering material riches is like sowing; in offering these riches, we will reap little if we sow little and reap much if we sow much (9:6, 10).

Day 6 XI. The giving and receiving of material things is intimately related to the experience of Christ (Phil. 4:10-20):

A. When we give and receive in the fellowship of life, there will be a blossoming in life (v. 10), the sign that life is flourishing, that there is a normal circulation of life in the Body of Christ.

B. The fellowship in the matters of giving and receiving not only ministers life to all concerned but brings all the parties into the glory of God (v. 19).

XII. **The word in Malachi 3:10 superabundantly displays the infinitely rich promise of God:**
   A. In principle, this word to the Israelites applies also to the New Testament believers.
   B. If we fully offer to God what belongs to Him that the church may be richly supplied, God will open the windows of heaven for us and pour out a blessing to us, which there will not be enough room to contain.

Morning Nourishment

1 John   Do not love the world nor the things in the world.
  2:15   If anyone loves the world, love for the Father is
         not in him.
  5:19   We know that we are of God, and the whole world
         lies in the evil one.
1 Tim.   Charge those who are rich in the present age not
  6:17   to be high-minded, nor to set their hope on the
         uncertainty of riches but on God, who affords us
         all things richly for *our* enjoyment.

From the time that man developed a problem with God because of the fall and left the position where he took God as everything, material riches have become a critical matter in the life of fallen man. In his fallen condition, man fell into the darkness of acknowledging only material riches and not God, of trusting only in material riches and not in God, and even of serving material riches, taking material riches as God, and allowing material riches to replace God. God's enemy, Satan, the devil, exploited the fallen condition of men to come in and deceive men to worship idols, such as the god of wealth, for riches and gain. By being behind these idols, he supplants men's worship and service that are due God. For this reason, the Lord Jesus told us that one "cannot serve God and mammon" (Matt. 6:24)....The service [mentioned] by the Lord here refers to the service of a slave....Satan utilizes material riches to seduce people to worship him on the one hand, and enslaves people in material riches...on the other hand. However, we have received God's mercy and the Lord's salvation, which delivered us from the authority of Satan and turned us to God (Acts 26:18). After we have received God's salvation in this way, we are confronted with an issue in our practical living, that is, what we should do with material riches that Satan used in time past to delude us and all the world. (*Life Lessons*, p. 99)

Today's Reading

The things that we need for our existence are earthly things, but they are not worldly things. What, then, are the worldly things? Just as the flesh is the corrupted body and the self is the corrupted soul, so the worldly things are the corrupted earthly things. Concerning the origin of the flesh, the self, and the world, the principle is the same.

The body has been corrupted by the sin of Satan and has become the flesh. The soul has been corrupted by the mind, the thought, of Satan and has become the self. The earthly things have been corrupted by Satan's systematic scheme and have become the world. The world is now a satanic system. In Greek this system is called the *kosmos*. In English this system is called the world.

We all need to have a clear vision of the world. To us the things which we need for our existence may simply be earthly things or they may become a world, a system of Satan. When you are preoccupied with eating, eating becomes an item of the world to you. When you are preoccupied with marriage, marriage becomes an item of the world to you. When you become preoccupied with clothing, housing, and transportation, these also become items of the world to you.

Are you clear about what the world is? Anything can become an item of the world to us, if that thing occupies us and preoccupies us. You need to be fully emancipated from every occupying and preoccupying thing....When this is your situation, you will have nothing to do with the world, yet you will still be living on the earth. You will continue to need food, marriage, clothing, housing, and transportation, but none of these things will occupy or preoccupy you.

If we see the vision of the world, we will realize that we should not love anything worldly. We should not love any occupying or preoccupying thing. Rather, we should give our love fully, wholly, and absolutely to the Lord. All our capacity is for Him. All the ground, all the room, in us is for Him. (*The Heavenly Vision,* pp. 51-53, 55-56)

Further Reading: Life Lessons, lsn. 24

Enlightenment and inspiration: _____

_____

_____

_____

Morning Nourishment

Luke And I say to you, Make friends for yourselves by
16:9 means of the mammon of unrighteousness, so that
when it fails, they may receive you into the eternal
tabernacles.

13 No household servant can serve two masters; for
either he will hate the one and love the other, or
he will hold to one and despise the other. You
cannot serve God and mammon.

Matthew 6:24 says, "No one can serve two masters, for either
he will hate the one and love the other, or he will hold to one
and despise the other. You cannot serve God and mammon."
The word *mammon* is an Aramaic word signifying wealth,
riches. Here mammon, standing in opposition to God, indicates
that wealth or riches is the opponent of God, robbing God's
people of their service to Him. (*Life-study of Matthew*, p. 272)

Today's Reading

The phrase *the mammon of unrighteousness* [in Luke 16:9]
indicates that money is not in the realm of God. Money is
outside the kingdom of God; it is in the world of Satan. Therefore, money is unrighteous both in position and existence.
Actually, as far as God is concerned, money should not exist. In
this universe there should not be such a thing as money. If we
love money, we love something that should not exist.

In verse 9 the Lord says that if we make friends by means
of the mammon of unrighteousness, when it fails we shall be
received into eternal tabernacles. The word *fails* indicates that
when the satanic world is over, mammon will be of no use in
the kingdom of God. The eternal tabernacles are the eternal
habitations into which the prudent believers will be received
by those who share the benefit of their prudence. This will be
in the coming kingdom age (Luke 14:13-14; Matt. 10:42).

In verse 12 the Lord goes on to say, "And if you have not
become faithful in that which belongs to another, who will give
to you that which is your own?" It is not God's intent in His New

Testament economy for the New Testament believers to care for material possessions. Though the material things in this world were created by God and belong to Him (1 Chron. 29:14,16), they have been corrupted by man's fall (Rom. 8:20-21) and usurped by Satan the evil one (1 John 5:19). Hence, they belong to fallen man and are unrighteous (Luke 16:9). While God does supply the believers with their daily necessities from the material things of this age (Matt. 6:31-33) and commits to them as His stewards a portion of these material goods for their exercise and learning that He may prove them in this age, none of these goods should be considered theirs until the restitution of all things in the next age (Acts 3:21). Not till then will the believers inherit the world (Rom. 4:13) and have an abiding possession (Heb. 10:34) for themselves. In this age they should exercise to be faithful in the temporary material things God has given them so that they may learn faithfulness toward their eternal possession in the coming age.

In Luke 16:13 the Greek word for *serve* means "serve as a slave." Here the Lord indicates that to serve Him requires us to love Him, giving our hearts to Him, and cleave to Him, giving our entire being to Him. Thus we are released from the occupation and usurpation of mammon so that we may serve the Lord wholly and fully. The Lord emphasizes here that to serve Him we must overcome the enticing deceitful mammon of unrighteousness.

In verse 13 we see that mammon is in rivalry with God, competing with Him. Because mammon is in rivalry with God, it is evil. On our part, we cannot serve two lords. We serve either God or mammon. This matter is very serious.

The Lord's word about money was directed especially to the Pharisees, who were lovers of money (v. 14). They pretended that they loved God and were for Him. But the Lord knew well that they were not lovers of God; they were lovers of money. (*Life-study of Luke,* pp. 308-310)

Further Reading: Life-study of Matthew, msg. 22; *Life-study of Luke,* msg. 36

Enlightenment and inspiration: _____

_____
_____
_____

Morning Nourishment

1 Cor. Now concerning the collection for the saints, just
16:1-3 as I directed the churches of Galatia, so you also
do. On the first day of the week each one of you
should lay aside in store to himself whatever he
may have been prospered, that no collections be
made when I come. And when I arrive, whomever
you approve, I will send them with letters to carry
your gift to Jerusalem.

Acts And the heart and soul of the multitude of those
4:32 who had believed was one; and not even one said
that any of his possessions was his own, but all
things were common to them.

In 1 Corinthians 15 Paul deals with the matter of resurrection. Then he opens chapter sixteen with a word about collecting material gifts on the first day of the week. The first day of the week signifies resurrection, for it is the day of resurrection.

The fact that material things are offered on the first day of the week indicates that they should be presented in resurrection, not in our natural life. Certain wealthy worldly people are able to write checks for large sums of money. But if they make a large donation, they usually make a name for themselves and advertise what they have done. This is not giving in resurrection. Our giving of money and material things must be in resurrection. This way of giving is a strong indication that we are under God's administration in resurrection and have overcome the possession of material things. As a result, God's administration will have a way to be carried on among us. (*Life-study of 1 Corinthians,* pp. 465-466)

Today's Reading

In 16:1 Paul says, "Now concerning the collection for the saints, just as I directed the churches of Galatia, so you also do." This is the eleventh matter dealt with by the apostle in this Epistle, a matter concerned with money, mammon, and material possessions. All of fallen mankind are under the domination of mammon and material possessions (Matt. 6:19-21, 24-25, 30; 19:21-22; Luke 12:13-19). At the day of Pentecost, under the power of the Holy Spirit, all the believers overthrew this domination and had all their possessions in common for distribution to the needy ones (Acts 2:44-45; 4:32, 34-37). That practice, due to the weakness of the believers' fallen nature (see Acts 5:1-11; 6:1), did not last long. It was already over by the apostle Paul's time. Then the believers needed grace to overcome the power of mammon and material things and to release them from Satan's domination for an offering to the Lord to fulfill His purpose. Resurrection life is the supply for the believers to live such a life, a life trusting in God, not in treasures of material possessions, a life not for today but for the future, not for this age but for the coming age (Luke 12:16-21; 1 Tim. 6:17-19), a life that overthrows the usurpation of temporal and uncertain riches....This dealing is related to God's administration among the churches.

It is a crucial matter that this dealing follows a chapter concerning the reality of resurrection life. Resurrection is not only the power over sin and death; resurrection is a power over mammon and material possessions. Therefore, immediately following the chapter on resurrection, Paul turns to the matter of material possessions. (*Life-study of 1 Corinthians,* pp. 625-626)

Acts 4:32 says, "...And not even one said that any of his possessions was his own, but all things were common to them." As in 2:44, having all things common was a sign not of love but of Christ's dynamic salvation that saved the believers from greed and selfishness. This was practiced for a short time at the initiation of God's New Testament economy; it did not continue for the long run as a practice of legality in the church life during Paul's ministry. (*Life-study of Acts,* p. 135)

Further Reading: Life-study of 1 Corinthians, msgs. 52, 69; *Life-study of Acts,* msg. 17

Enlightenment and inspiration: _____

_____

_____

_____

Morning Nourishment

1 Cor. On the first day of the week each one of you should
16:2-3 lay aside in store to himself whatever he may have
been prospered, that no collections be made when
I come. And when I arrive, whomever you approve,
I will send them with letters to carry your gift to
Jerusalem.

Matt. But you, when you give alms, do not let your left
6:3-4 hand know what your right hand is doing, so that
your alms may be in secret; and your Father who
sees in secret will repay you.

The seventh day of the week, the Sabbath, was a memorial
of God's creation (Gen. 2:1-3; Exo. 20:8, 11). The first day of the
week is a symbol of the Lord's resurrection; it is the day the
Lord resurrected from among the dead (John 20:1). It is called
the Lord's Day (Rev. 1:10). The New Testament saints meet and
offer their possessions on this day (Acts 20:7[; 1 Cor. 16:2]), the
day of the Lord's resurrection, signifying that they have been
resurrected with the Lord (Eph. 2:6) through His resurrection
(1 Pet. 1:3), and that they meet to remember Him and worship
God with their offerings in resurrection by the resurrection life,
not by their natural life.

Our giving must be in resurrection life, not in our natural life.
However, much of the giving by Christians today is done according to the natural life. Money is raised by the natural life in a way
that is absolutely in the old creation. Furthermore, those who give
large amounts are often publicly recognized, whereas those who
give small amounts are ignored. Our giving must be completely
different from this. Our offerings must be presented in resurrection and by resurrection. (*Life-study of 1 Corinthians,* p. 626)

Today's Reading

The Greek word rendered *gift* [in 1 Corinthians 16:3] can
also be translated *grace*. This was a kind of fellowship, under
the apostle's direction, of the churches in the Gentile world with
the church in Jerusalem (2 Cor. 8:1-2; Rom. 15:25-27).

[In 1 Corinthians 11 through 16], Paul deals with matters in the realm of the divine administration. This section begins with the headship of God and consummates with a seemingly insignificant matter—the gift of material things for the saints. Whether or not we are truly in God's administration, or for God's administration, and are carrying out God's administration, can be tested by how we are related to material things and how we handle our money. If we use our money in a worldly way, then no matter what we may say about resurrection, we are not truly in God's administration. The extent to which we are in the divine administration and for the divine administration is determined by how we care for money and material possessions.

Throughout the years, we in the Lord's recovery have been hearing His Word and have been built up in the riches of Christ. We have surely been nourished by the divine Word. Now if we all would be faithful to live for God's administration in caring for money and material matters, there would be no financial needs in the recovery. For example, certainly we can exercise our spirit and our will to save a small amount of money each week, perhaps just two dollars and fifty cents, and give this to the Lord for His move on earth. One day, instead of having our lunch at a restaurant, we may eat a simple meal prepared at home. Then the money saved could be given to the Lord. Imagine what the situation would be if we all were faithful to do something like this week by week!

In such a spiritual book dealing with spiritual and heavenly matters, Paul eventually turns to the very practical matter of finances....It is easy for our talk to be abstract and impractical concerning the headship, discerning the Body, the gifts, and resurrection. For this reason, Paul, in God's wisdom, deals with the matter of giving immediately after the matter of resurrection. If we truly live in resurrection, we shall not have a problem with money or material things. (*Life-study of 1 Corinthians,* pp. 627-628)

Further Reading: Life-study of 1 Corinthians, msg. 69

Enlightenment and inspiration: _____

_____

_____

_____

Morning Nourishment

Luke   And I say to you, Make friends for yourselves by
16:9   means of the mammon of unrighteousness, so
       that when it fails, they may receive you into the
       eternal tabernacles.

6:38   Give, and it will be given to you; a good measure,
       pressed down, shaken together, *and* running
       over, they will give into your bosom. For with
       what measure you measure, it shall be measured
       to you in return.

Acts   ...It is more blessed to give than to receive.
20:35

"Remember the words of the Lord Jesus, that He Himself said,
It is more blessed to give than to receive" (Acts 20:35). Concerning
material riches, human beings, who are deceived by Satan, will
only receive and not give. To want to receive and not give is Satan's
ploy, which causes man to lose God's blessing. The best way to be
blessed by God in material riches is to give, not to receive, just as
the Lord Himself did for us. Thus, the Lord Himself promised us
that it is more blessed to give than to receive. Myriads of believers
throughout the ages who have believed in the Lord's word and
who have practiced accordingly confirm the trustworthiness of
this promise from their experience. (*Life Lessons,* p. 102)

Today's Reading

[Luke 16:9] indicates that those who have been benefited by
our proper use of money will welcome us into the eternal
tabernacles. This will be in the coming age of the kingdom.
When the Lord Jesus comes back and we are received into His
kingdom, some of us will have a number of people welcoming
us. Who will be these welcomers? They will be those who have
received benefit in this age by our prudent use of money.

Suppose you use an amount of your money to publish gospel
tracts for the purpose of bringing people to the Lord. Those who
have been benefited by this use of your money will welcome you
in the future. They may say, "Brother, we want you to realize

that we were saved through one of the tracts paid for by you." This is an example of being welcomed into eternal habitations by those who have shared the benefit of our prudence.

I would encourage the young people in particular to learn to give a portion of their income to the Lord....Give a portion of the first wages you receive to the Lord. I can testify that this was my practice....When I first earned money, even as a poor student, I set aside a portion to the Lord....If we do this, we shall learn to handle our money properly.

Those who give to the Lord faithfully and consistently can testify that the more they give, the more they receive. For us Christians, to be rich is to give. The way to receive is to give. The Lord Himself said, "Give, and it will be given to you; a good measure, pressed down, shaken together, and running over, they will give into your bosom. For with what measure you measure, it shall be measured to you in return" (6:38). Here we see clearly that giving is the way to receive.

For a church to be in poverty is a shame to the members of that church. Such poverty may indicate that the members are not faithful in their giving. May we all learn to serve the Lord as faithful stewards in handling money.

I encourage you to keep a record of your giving. During the course of a year, keep a record of everything you give. Then at the end of the year consider what percentage you have given to the Lord of what He has given you. I urge you all to practice this.

According to the statistics I have studied and the testimonies I have heard, the more we give to the Lord, the more we shall be able to give. For example, if you give ten percent one year, the next year you may be able to give twenty percent. Then if you are faithful to give a higher amount, you may be able to give even more the following year. The point here is that the more we give, the more we shall be able to give. (*Life-study of Luke,* pp. 313-316)

Further Reading: Life Lessons, lsn. 24; *Life-study of Luke,*
   msgs. 15, 29, 36

Enlightenment and inspiration: _____

_____
_____
_____

Morning Nourishment

Mal. Bring the whole tithe to the storehouse that there
3:10 may be food in My house; and prove Me, if you will,
by this, says Jehovah of hosts, whether I will open
to you the windows of heaven and pour out blessing for you until there is no room for it.

Phil. But I rejoiced in the Lord greatly because now at
4:10 length you have caused your thinking for me to
blossom anew; for which matter you had indeed
taken thought, but lacked opportunity.

15 And you yourselves also know, Philippians, that in
the beginning of the gospel, when I went out from
Macedonia, no church had fellowship with me in
the account of giving and receiving except you only.

19 And my God will fill your every need according to
His riches, in glory, in Christ Jesus.

[Malachi 3:10] superabundantly displays the infinitely rich
promise of God. Although it was spoken to the Israelites in the
Old Testament, in principle it applies also to the New Testament believers. If we will fully offer to God what belongs to Him
that the church may be richly supplied, God will open the
windows of heaven for us and pour out a blessing to us, which
there will not be enough room to contain. This is a solemn
promise of the Lord of hosts. We can offer to Him according to
His promise to prove Him. (*Life Lessons,* p. 103)

Today's Reading

According to the Bible, fellowship always comes from life.
First John 1:2 and 3 reveal that fellowship issues from life. The
source of fellowship is life. For this reason, in Philippians 4:10
Paul uses the word *blossom,* and in verse 14, the word *fellowship:* "Nevertheless you did well to have fellowship with me in
my affliction." It seems as if Paul is saying, "You ministered life
to me and helped to sustain me in my imprisonment. When I
was suffering, you helped me by ministering life to me. Surely
you will receive a supply of life in return."

In [Philippians 4:10 and 14-20] Paul speaks of blossoming, fellowship, a sacrifice to God, a sweet odor, and God supplying every need according to His riches in glory in Christ Jesus. All these terms and expressions indicate that even the giving and receiving of material things is intimately related to the experience of Christ. On our side, it is related to life; on God's side, it is related to His glory. We give and receive in the way of life, in the fellowship of life. When we do this, there will be the blossoming in life, the sign that life is flourishing, that there is a normal circulation of life in the Body of Christ. The issue of this giving and receiving in the fellowship of life is the glory of God.

In giving to the apostle, the believers participated in the ministry of life. Paul's answer upon receiving their gift was also a ministry of life, both to the believers in Philippi and to all the saints who read this portion of the Word. By this we see that even the giving and receiving of material gifts can become a rich experience of Christ which issues in the glorification of God. God comes in to visit both the ones who give and the one who receives in such a way as to express His splendor, His glory. Thus, the fellowship in the matters of giving and receiving not only ministers life to all concerned, but also brings all parties into the glory of God.

The matter of giving and receiving in the way described in Philippians 4 is not a matter of natural generosity, of donating something out of a willingness to sacrifice. No, what is described here is an actual experience of Christ. If we give according to Paul's word, we give not in ourselves, but in Christ. When our gift is presented in Christ and through Christ, it becomes something of life that blossoms. Furthermore, it becomes a sweet odor, a sacrifice well pleasing to God. This will cause God's glory to be manifested to us. This is the experience of Christ in giving material things for the Lord's interest. (*Life-study of Philippians*, pp. 256-257, 262-263, 265)

Further Reading: Life-study of Philippians, msg. 30

Enlightenment and inspiration: _____

_____

_____

_____

Hymns, #438

1   I've turned my back upon the world
    With all its idle pleasures,
And set my heart on better things,
    On higher, holier treasures;
No more its glitter and its glare,
    And vanity shall blind me;
I've crossed the separating line,
    And left the world behind me.

    Far, far behind me!
    Far, far behind me!
I've crossed the separating line,
    And left the world behind me.

2   I've left the old sad life of sin,
    Its follies all forsaken;
My standing place is now in Christ,
    His holy vows I've taken;
Beneath the standard of the cross
    The world henceforth shall find me;
I've passed in Christ from death to life,
    And left the world behind me.

    Far, far behind me!
    Far, far behind me!
I've passed in Christ from death to life,
    And left the world behind me.

3   My soul shall ne'er return again
    Back to its former station,
For here alone is perfect peace,
    And rest from condemnation;
I've made exchange of masters now,
    The vows of glory bind me,
And once for all I've left the world,
    Yes, left the world behind me.

    Far, far behind me!
    Far, far behind me!
And once for all I've left the world,
    Yes, left the world behind me.

4   My choice is made forevermore,
      I want no other Savior;
    I ask no purer happiness
      Than His sweet love and favor;
    My heart is fixed on Jesus Christ,
      No more the world shall blind me;
    I've crossed the Red Sea of His death,
      And left the world behind me.

       Far, far behind me!
       Far, far behind me!
    I've crossed the Red Sea of His death,
      And left the world behind me.

Composition for prophecy with main point and sub-points: _____

_____

_____

_____

_____

_____

_____

_____

_____

_____

_____

_____

_____

_____

_____

_____

_____

_____

_____

_____

_____

_____

_____

_____

_____

_____

Reading Schedule for the Recovery Version of the New Testament with Footnotes

Wk.	Lord's Day	Monday	Tuesday	Wednesday	Thursday	Friday	Saturday
1	☐ Matt 1:1-2	☐ 1:3-7	☐ 1:8-17	☐ 1:18-25	☐ 2:1-23	☐ 3:1-6	☐ 3:7-17
2	☐ 4:1-11	☐ 4:12-25	☐ 5:1-4	☐ 5:5-12	☐ 5:13-20	☐ 5:21-26	☐ 5:27-48
3	☐ 6:1-8	☐ 6:9-18	☐ 6:19-34	☐ 7:1-12	☐ 7:13-29	☐ 8:1-13	☐ 8:14-22
4	☐ 8:23-34	☐ 9:1-13	☐ 9:14-17	☐ 9:18-34	☐ 9:35—10:5	☐ 10:6-25	☐ 10:26-42
5	☐ 11:1-15	☐ 11:16-30	☐ 12:1-14	☐ 12:15-32	☐ 12:33-42	☐ 12:43—13:2	☐ 13:3-12
6	☐ 13:13-30	☐ 13:31-43	☐ 13:44-58	☐ 14:1-13	☐ 14:14-21	☐ 14:22-36	☐ 15:1-20
7	☐ 15:21-31	☐ 15:32-39	☐ 16:1-12	☐ 16:13-20	☐ 16:21-28	☐ 17:1-13	☐ 17:14-27
8	☐ 18:1-14	☐ 18:15-22	☐ 18:23-35	☐ 19:1-15	☐ 19:16-30	☐ 20:1-16	☐ 20:17-34
9	☐ 21:1-11	☐ 21:12-22	☐ 21:23-32	☐ 21:33-46	☐ 22:1-22	☐ 22:23-33	☐ 22:34-46
10	☐ 23:1-12	☐ 23:13-39	☐ 24:1-14	☐ 24:15-31	☐ 24:32-51	☐ 25:1-13	☐ 25:14-30
11	☐ 25:31-46	☐ 26:1-16	☐ 26:17-35	☐ 26:36-46	☐ 26:47-64	☐ 26:65-75	☐ 27:1-26
12	☐ 27:27-44	☐ 27:45-56	☐ 27:57—28:15	☐ 28:16-20	☐ Mark 1:1	☐ 1:2-6	☐ 1:7-13
13	☐ 1:14-28	☐ 1:29-45	☐ 2:1-12	☐ 2:13-28	☐ 3:1-19	☐ 3:20-35	☐ 4:1-25
14	☐ 4:26-41	☐ 5:1-20	☐ 5:21-43	☐ 6:1-29	☐ 6:30-56	☐ 7:1-23	☐ 7:24-37
15	☐ 8:1-26	☐ 8:27—9:1	☐ 9:2-29	☐ 9:30-50	☐ 10:1-16	☐ 10:17-34	☐ 10:35-52
16	☐ 11:1-16	☐ 11:17-33	☐ 12:1-27	☐ 12:28-44	☐ 13:1-13	☐ 13:14-37	☐ 14:1-26
17	☐ 14:27-52	☐ 14:53-72	☐ 15:1-15	☐ 15:16-47	☐ 16:1-8	☐ 16:9-20	☐ Luke 1:1-4
18	☐ 1:5-25	☐ 1:26-46	☐ 1:47-56	☐ 1:57-80	☐ 2:1-8	☐ 2:9-20	☐ 2:21-39
19	☐ 2:40-52	☐ 3:1-20	☐ 3:21-38	☐ 4:1-13	☐ 4:14-30	☐ 4:31-44	☐ 5:1-26
20	☐ 5:27—6:16	☐ 6:17-38	☐ 6:39-49	☐ 7:1-17	☐ 7:18-23	☐ 7:24-35	☐ 7:36-50
21	☐ 8:1-15	☐ 8:16-25	☐ 8:26-39	☐ 8:40-56	☐ 9:1-17	☐ 9:18-26	☐ 9:27-36
22	☐ 9:37-50	☐ 9:51-62	☐ 10:1-11	☐ 10:12-24	☐ 10:25-37	☐ 10:38-42	☐ 11:1-13
23	☐ 11:14-26	☐ 11:27-36	☐ 11:37-54	☐ 12:1-12	☐ 12:13-21	☐ 12:22-34	☐ 12:35-48
24	☐ 12:49-59	☐ 13:1-9	☐ 13:10-17	☐ 13:18-30	☐ 13:31—14:6	☐ 14:7-14	☐ 14:15-24
25	☐ 14:25-35	☐ 15:1-10	☐ 15:11-21	☐ 15:22-32	☐ 16:1-13	☐ 16:14-22	☐ 16:23-31
26	☐ 17:1-19	☐ 17:20-37	☐ 18:1-14	☐ 18:15-30	☐ 18:31-43	☐ 19:1-10	☐ 19:11-27

Reading Schedule for the Recovery Version of the New Testament with Footnotes

Wk.	Lord's Day	Monday	Tuesday	Wednesday	Thursday	Friday	Saturday
27	□ Luke 19:28-48	□ 20:1-19	□ 20:20-38	□ 20:39—21:4	□ 21:5-27	□ 21:28-38	□ 22:1-20
28	□ 22:21-38	□ 22:39-54	□ 22:55-71	□ 23:1-43	□ 23:44-56	□ 24:1-12	□ 24:13-35
29	□ 24:36-53	□ John 1:1-13	□ 1:14-18	□ 1:19-34	□ 1:35-51	□ 2:1-11	□ 2:12-22
30	□ 2:23—3:13	□ 3:14-21	□ 3:22-36	□ 4:1-14	□ 4:15-26	□ 4:27-42	□ 4:43-54
31	□ 5:1-16	□ 5:17-30	□ 5:31-47	□ 6:1-15	□ 6:16-31	□ 6:32-51	□ 6:52-71
32	□ 7:1-9	□ 7:10-24	□ 7:25-36	□ 7:37-52	□ 7:53—8:11	□ 8:12-27	□ 8:28-44
33	□ 8:45-59	□ 9:1-13	□ 9:14-34	□ 9:35—10:9	□ 10:10-30	□ 10:31—11:4	□ 11:5-22
34	□ 11:23-40	□ 11:41-57	□ 12:1-11	□ 12:12-24	□ 12:25-36	□ 12:37-50	□ 13:1-11
35	□ 13:12-30	□ 13:31-38	□ 14:1-6	□ 14:7-20	□ 14:21-31	□ 15:1-11	□ 15:12-27
36	□ 16:1-15	□ 16:16-33	□ 17:1-5	□ 17:6-13	□ 17:14-24	□ 17:25—18:11	□ 18:12-27
37	□ 18:28-40	□ 19:1-16	□ 19:17-30	□ 19:31-42	□ 20:1-13	□ 20:14-18	□ 20:19-22
38	□ 20:23-31	□ 21:1-14	□ 21:15-22	□ 21:23-25	□ Acts 1:1-8	□ 1:9-14	□ 1:15-26
39	□ 2:1-13	□ 2:14-21	□ 2:22-36	□ 2:37-41	□ 2:42-47	□ 3:1-18	□ 3:19—4:22
40	□ 4:23-37	□ 5:1-16	□ 5:17-32	□ 5:33-42	□ 6:1—7:1	□ 7:2-29	□ 7:30-60
41	□ 8:1-13	□ 8:14-25	□ 8:26-40	□ 9:1-19	□ 9:20-43	□ 10:1-16	□ 10:17-33
42	□ 10:34-48	□ 11:1-18	□ 11:19-30	□ 12:1-25	□ 13:1-12	□ 13:13-43	□ 13:44—14:5
43	□ 14:6-28	□ 15:1-12	□ 15:13-34	□ 15:35—16:5	□ 16:6-18	□ 16:19-40	□ 17:1-18
44	□ 17:19-34	□ 18:1-17	□ 18:18-28	□ 19:1-20	□ 19:21-41	□ 20:1-12	□ 20:13-38
45	□ 21:1-14	□ 21:15-26	□ 21:27-40	□ 22:1-21	□ 22:22-29	□ 22:30—23:11	□ 23:12-15
46	□ 23:16-30	□ 23:31—24:21	□ 24:22—25:5	□ 25:6-27	□ 26:1-13	□ 26:14-32	□ 27:1-26
47	□ 27:27—28:10	□ 28:11-22	□ 28:23-31	□ Rom 1:1-2	□ 1:3-7	□ 1:8-17	□ 1:18-25
48	□ 1:26—2:10	□ 2:11-29	□ 3:1-20	□ 3:21-31	□ 4:1-12	□ 4:13-25	□ 5:1-11
49	□ 5:12-17	□ 5:18—6:5	□ 6:6-11	□ 6:12-23	□ 7:1-12	□ 7:13-25	□ 8:1-2
50	□ 8:3-6	□ 8:7-13	□ 8:14-25	□ 8:26-39	□ 9:1-18	□ 9:19—10:3	□ 10:4-15
51	□ 10:16—11:10	□ 11:11-22	□ 11:23-36	□ 12:1-3	□ 12:4-21	□ 13:1-14	□ 14:1-12
52	□ 14:13-23	□ 15:1-13	□ 15:14-33	□ 16:1-5	□ 16:6-24	□ 16:25-27	□ I Cor 1:1-4

Reading Schedule for the Recovery Version of the New Testament with Footnotes

Wk.	Lord's Day	Monday	Tuesday	Wednesday	Thursday	Friday	Saturday
53	☐ I Cor 1:5-9	☐ 1:10-17	☐ 1:18-31	☐ 2:1-5	☐ 2:6-10	☐ 2:11-16	☐ 3:1-9
54	☐ 3:10-13	☐ 3:14-23	☐ 4:1-9	☐ 4:10-21	☐ 5:1-13	☐ 6:1-11	☐ 6:12-20
55	☐ 7:1-16	☐ 7:17-24	☐ 7:25-40	☐ 8:1-13	☐ 9:1-15	☐ 9:16-27	☐ 10:1-4
56	☐ 10:5-13	☐ 10:14-33	☐ 11:1-6	☐ 11:7-16	☐ 11:17-26	☐ 11:27-34	☐ 12:1-11
57	☐ 12:12-22	☐ 12:23-31	☐ 13:1-13	☐ 14:1-12	☐ 14:13-25	☐ 14:26-33	☐ 14:34-40
58	☐ 15:1-19	☐ 15:20-28	☐ 15:29-34	☐ 15:35-49	☐ 15:50-58	☐ 16:1-9	☐ 16:10-24
59	☐ II Cor 1:1-4	☐ 1:5-14	☐ 1:15-22	☐ 1:23—2:11	☐ 2:12-17	☐ 3:1-6	☐ 3:7-11
60	☐ 3:12-18	☐ 4:1-6	☐ 4:7-12	☐ 4:13-18	☐ 5:1-8	☐ 5:9-15	☐ 5:16-21
61	☐ 6:1-13	☐ 6:14—7:4	☐ 7:5-16	☐ 8:1-15	☐ 8:16-24	☐ 9:1-15	☐ 10:1-6
62	☐ 10:7-18	☐ 11:1-15	☐ 11:16-33	☐ 12:1-10	☐ 12:11-21	☐ 13:1-10	☐ 13:11-14
63	☐ Gal 1:1-5	☐ 1:6-14	☐ 1:15-24	☐ 2:1-13	☐ 2:14-21	☐ 3:1-4	☐ 3:5-14
64	☐ 3:15-22	☐ 3:23-29	☐ 4:1-7	☐ 4:8-20	☐ 4:21-31	☐ 5:1-12	☐ 5:13-21
65	☐ 5:22-26	☐ 6:1-10	☐ 6:11-15	☐ 6:16-18	☐ Eph 1:1-3	☐ 1:4-6	☐ 1:7-10
66	☐ 1:11-14	☐ 1:15-18	☐ 1:19-23	☐ 2:1-5	☐ 2:6-10	☐ 2:11-14	☐ 2:15-18
67	☐ 2:19-22	☐ 3:1-7	☐ 3:8-13	☐ 3:14-18	☐ 3:19-21	☐ 4:1-4	☐ 4:5-10
68	☐ 4:11-16	☐ 4:17-24	☐ 4:25-32	☐ 5:1-10	☐ 5:11-21	☐ 5:22-26	☐ 5:27-33
69	☐ 6:1-9	☐ 6:10-14	☐ 6:15-18	☐ 6:19-24	☐ Phil 1:1-7	☐ 1:8-18	☐ 1:19-26
70	☐ 1:27—2:4	☐ 2:5-11	☐ 2:12-16	☐ 2:17-30	☐ 3:1-6	☐ 3:7-11	☐ 3:12-16
71	☐ 3:17-21	☐ 4:1-9	☐ 4:10-23	☐ Col 1:1-8	☐ 1:9-13	☐ 1:14-23	☐ 1:24-29
72	☐ 2:1-7	☐ 2:8-15	☐ 2:16-23	☐ 3:1-4	☐ 3:5-15	☐ 3:16-25	☐ 4:1-18
73	☐ I Thes 1:1-3	☐ 1:4-10	☐ 2:1-12	☐ 2:13—3:5	☐ 3:6-13	☐ 4:1-10	☐ 4:11—5:11
74	☐ 5:12-28	☐ II Thes 1:1-12	☐ 2:1-17	☐ 3:1-18	☐ I Tim 1:1-2	☐ 1:3-4	☐ 1:5-14
75	☐ 1:15-20	☐ 2:1-7	☐ 2:8-15	☐ 3:1-13	☐ 3:14—4:5	☐ 4:6-16	☐ 5:1-25
76	☐ 6:1-10	☐ 6:11-21	☐ II Tim 1:1-10	☐ 1:11-18	☐ 2:1-15	☐ 2:16-26	☐ 3:1-13
77	☐ 3:14—4:8	☐ 4:9-22	☐ Titus 1:1-4	☐ 1:5-16	☐ 2:1-15	☐ 3:1-8	☐ 3:9-15
78	☐ Philem 1:1-11	☐ 1:12-25	☐ Heb 1:1-2	☐ 1:3-5	☐ 1:6-14	☐ 2:1-9	☐ 2:10-18

Reading Schedule for the Recovery Version of the New Testament with Footnotes

Wk.	Lord's Day	Monday	Tuesday	Wednesday	Thursday	Friday	Saturday
79	Heb 3:1-6	3:7-19	4:1-9	4:10-13	4:14-16	5:1-10	5:11—6:3
80	6:4-8	6:9-20	7:1-10	7:11-28	8:1-6	8:7-13	9:1-4
81	9:5-14	9:15-28	10:1-18	10:19-28	10:29-39	11:1-6	11:7-19
82	11:20-31	11:32-40	12:1-2	12:3-13	12:14-17	12:18-26	12:27-29
83	13:1-7	13:8-12	13:13-15	13:16-25	James1:1-8	1:9-18	1:19-27
84	2:1-13	2:14-26	3:1-18	4:1-10	4:11-17	5:1-12	5:13-20
85	I Pet 1:1-2	1:3-4	1:5	1:6-9	1:10-12	1:13-17	1:18-25
86	2:1-3	2:4-8	2:9-17	2:18-25	3:1-13	3:14-22	4:1-6
87	4:7-16	4:17-19	5:1-4	5:5-9	5:10-14	II Pet 1:1-2	1:3-4
88	1:5-8	1:9-11	1:12-18	1:19-21	2:1-3	2:4-11	2:12-22
89	3:1-6	3:7-9	3:10-12	3:13-15	3:16	3:17-18	I John 1:1-2
90	1:3-4	1:5	1:6	1:7	1:8-10	2:1-2	2:3-11
91	2:12-14	2:15-19	2:20-23	2:24-27	2:28-29	3:1-5	3:6-10
92	3:11-18	3:19-24	4:1-6	4:7-11	4:12-15	4:16—5:3	5:4-13
93	5:14-17	5:18-21	II John 1:1-3	1:4-9	1:10-13	III John 1:1-6	1:7-14
94	Jude 1:1-4	1:5-10	1:11-19	1:20-25	Rev 1:1-3	1:4-6	1:7-11
95	1:12-13	1:14-16	1:17-20	2:1-6	2:7	2:8-9	2:10-11
96	2:12-14	2:15-17	2:18-23	2:24-29	3:1-3	3:4-6	3:7-9
97	3:10-13	3:14-18	3:19-22	4:1-5	4:6-7	4:8-11	5:1-6
98	5:7-14	6:1-8	6:9-17	7:1-8	7:9-17	8:1-6	8:7-12
99	8:13—9:11	9:12-21	10:1-4	10:5-11	11:1-4	11:5-14	11:15-19
100	12:1-4	12:5-9	12:10-18	13:1-10	13:11-18	14:1-5	14:6-12
101	14:13-20	15:1-8	16:1-12	16:13-21	17:1-6	17:7-18	18:1-8
102	18:9—19:4	19:5-10	19:11-16	19:17-21	20:1-6	20:7-10	20:11-15
103	21:1	21:2	21:3-8	21:9-13	21:14-18	21:19-21	21:22-27
104	22:1	22:2	22:3-11	22:12-15	22:16-17	22:18-21	

Week 7 — Day 4 — Today's verses

1 Cor. 10:21 You cannot drink the Lord's cup and the demons' cup; you cannot partake of the Lord's table and of the demons' table.

Deut. 8:7 For Jehovah your God is bringing you to a good land, a land of waterbrooks, of springs and of fountains, flowing forth in valleys and in mountains.

9-10 A land in which you will eat bread without scarcity; you will not lack anything in it; a land whose stones are iron, and from whose mountains you can mine copper. And you shall eat and be satisfied, and you shall bless Jehovah your God for the good land which He has given you.

Date _____

Week 7 — Day 5 — Today's verses

1 Cor. 11:23-26 For I received from the Lord that which also I delivered to you, that the Lord Jesus in the night in which He was betrayed took bread, and having given thanks, He broke it and said, This is My body, which is *given* for you; this do unto the remembrance of Me. Similarly also the cup after they had dined, saying, This cup is the new covenant *established* in My blood; this do, as often as you drink *it*, unto the remembrance of Me. For as often as you eat this bread and drink the cup, you declare the Lord's death until He comes.

Date _____

Week 7 — Day 6 — Today's verses

1 Cor. 11:26 For as often as you eat this bread and drink the cup, you declare the Lord's death until He comes.

29 For he who eats and drinks, eats and drinks judgment to himself if he does not discern the body.

Matt. 26:29 But I say to you, I shall by no means drink of this product of the vine from now on until that day when I drink it new with you in the kingdom of My Father.

Date _____

Week 7 — Day 1 — Today's verses

Gen. 2:9 And out of the ground Jehovah God caused to grow every tree that is pleasant to the sight and good for food, as well as the tree of life in the middle of the garden and the tree of the knowledge of good and evil.

Rev. 2:7 ...To him who overcomes, to him I will give to eat of the tree of life, which is in the Paradise of God.

22:14 Blessed are those who wash their robes that they may have right to the tree of life and may enter by the gates into the city.

Date _____

Week 7 — Day 2 — Today's verses

1 Cor. 10:3-4 And all ate the same spiritual food, and all drank the same spiritual drink; for they drank of a spiritual rock which followed *them*, and the rock was Christ.

14 Therefore, my beloved, flee from idolatry.

Num. 11:6 But now our appetite has gone; there is nothing at all but this manna to look at.

Date _____

Week 7 — Day 3 — Today's verses

1 Cor. 10:16-17 The cup of blessing which we bless, is it not the fellowship of the blood of Christ? The bread which we break, is it not the fellowship of the body of Christ? Seeing that there is one bread, we who are many are one Body; for we all partake of the one bread.

1:9 God is faithful, through whom you were called into the fellowship of His Son, Jesus Christ our Lord.

Date _____

Week 8 — Day 6   Today's verses

1 Cor. To the church of God which is in
1:2   Corinth…
7:17   …And so I direct in all the churches.
11:16   …We do not have such a custom of being
so, neither the churches of God.
12:27   Now you are the Body of Christ, and
members individually.
14:33   …As in all the churches of the saints.
Eph.   In whom you also are being built together
2:22   into a dwelling place of God in spirit.
4:4   One Body and one Spirit…
Rev.   Saying, What you see write in a scroll and
1:11   send it to the seven churches…

Date

Week 8 — Day 3   Today's verses

1 Cor. That there would be no division in the
12:25   body, but that the members would have
the same care for one another.
Eph.   Being diligent to keep the oneness of the
4:3   Spirit in the uniting bond of peace.
13   Until we all arrive at the oneness of the
faith and of the full knowledge of the Son
of God, at a full-grown man, at the measure of the stature of the fullness of Christ.

Date

Week 8 — Day 5   Today's verses

1 Cor. But our comely members have no need.
12:24-25   But God has blended the body together,
giving more abundant honor to the member that lacked, that there would be no
division in the body, but that the members would have the same care for one
another.
1 John   That which we have seen and heard we
1:3   report also to you that you also may have
fellowship with us, and indeed our fellowship is with the Father and with His
Son Jesus Christ.

Date

Week 8 — Day 2   Today's verses

1 Cor. For he who eats and drinks, eats and
11:29   drinks judgment to himself if he does not
discern the body.
Eph.   And He subjected all things under His
1:22-23   feet and gave Him to be Head over all
things to the church, which is His Body,
the fullness of the One who fills all in all.

Date

Week 8 — Day 4   Today's verses

1 Cor. For even as the body is one and has many
12:12-13   members, yet all the members of the
body, being many, are one body, so also
is the Christ. For also in one Spirit we
were all baptized into one Body, whether
Jews or Greeks, whether slaves or free,
and were all given to drink one Spirit.

Date

Week 8 — Day 1   Today's verses

1 Cor. To the church of God which is in
1:2   Corinth…with all those who call upon
the name of our Lord Jesus Christ in every
place, who is theirs and ours.
11:3   But I want you to know that Christ is the
head of every man, and the man is the
head of the woman, and God is the head
of Christ.
12:27   Now you are the Body of Christ, and
members individually.

Date

Week 9 — Day 1 Today's verses

Eph. 5:29 For no one ever hated his own flesh, but nourishes and cherishes it, even as Christ also the church.

Matt. 9:12 ...He said, Those who are strong have no need of a physician, but those who are ill.

1 Cor. 12:31 ...And moreover I show to you a most excellent way.

13:7-8 [Love] covers all things....Love never falls away....

14:1 Pursue love...

8:1 ...Knowledge puffs up, but love builds up.

_____
Date

Week 9 — Day 2 Today's verses

1 John 4:8 He who does not love has not known God, because God is love.

John 3:16 For God so loved the world that He gave His only begotten Son, that every one who believes into Him would not perish, but would have eternal life.

Matt. 5:44-45 But I say to you, Love your enemies, and pray for those who persecute you, so that you may become sons of your Father who is in the heavens, because He causes His sun to rise on the evil and the good and sends rain on the just and the unjust.

_____
Date

Week 9 — Day 3 Today's verses

1 Cor. 8:1-3 Now concerning things sacrificed to idols, we know that we all have knowledge. Knowledge puffs up, but love builds up. If anyone thinks that he knows anything, he has not yet come to know as he ought to know; but if anyone loves God, this one is known by Him.

Matt. 7:23 And then I will declare to them: I never knew you. Depart from Me, you workers of lawlessness.

_____
Date

Week 9 — Day 4 Today's verses

1 Cor. 13:4-8 Love suffers long. Love is kind; it is not jealous. Love does not brag and is not puffed up; it does not behave unbecomingly and does not seek its own things; it is not provoked and does not take account of evil; it does not rejoice because of unrighteousness, but rejoices with the truth; it covers all things, believes all things, hopes all things, endures all things. Love never falls away. But whether prophecies, they will be rendered useless; or tongues, they will cease; or knowledge, it will be rendered useless.

_____
Date

Week 9 — Day 5 Today's verses

Eph. 4:16 Out from whom all the Body...causes the growth of the Body unto the building up of itself in love.

2 Tim. 1:7 For God has not given us a spirit of cowardice, but of power and of love and of sobermindedness.

2:22 But flee youthful lusts, and pursue righteousness, faith, love, peace with those who call on the Lord out of a pure heart.

1 John 3:14 We know that we have passed out of death into life because we love the brothers. He who does not love abides in death.

_____
Date

Week 9 — Day 6 Today's verses

2 Pet. 1:4 Through which He has granted to us precious and exceedingly great promises that through these you might become partakers of the divine nature, having escaped the corruption which is in the world by lust.

1 John 4:16 And we know and have believed the love which God has in us. God is love, and he who abides in love abides in God and God abides in him.

1:3 That which we have seen and heard we report also to you that you also may have fellowship with us, and indeed our fellowship is with the Father and with His Son Jesus Christ.

_____
Date

Week 10 — Day 4 — Today's verses

1 Cor. 14:1 — Pursue love, and desire earnestly spiritual *gifts*, but especially that you may prophesy.

12 — So also you, since you are zealous of spirits, seek that you may excel for the building up of the church.

31 — For you can all prophesy one by one that all may learn and all may be encouraged.

39 — So then, my brothers, desire earnestly the prophesying…

_____
Date

Week 10 — Day 5 — Today's verses

1 Cor. 14:26 — What then, brothers? Whenever you come together, each one has a psalm, has a teaching, has a revelation, has a tongue, has an interpretation. Let all things be done for building up.

Heb. 10:24-25 — And let us consider one another so as to incite *one another* to love and good works, not abandoning our own assembling together, as the custom with some is, but exhorting *one another*; and so much the more as you see the day drawing near.

_____
Date

Week 10 — Day 6 — Today's verses

Col. 3:16 — Let the word of Christ dwell in you richly in all wisdom, teaching and admonishing one another with psalms *and* hymns *and* spiritual songs, singing with grace in your hearts to God.

Acts 5:20 — Go and stand in the temple and speak to the people all the words of this life.

1 Cor. 14:32 — And the spirits of prophets are subject to prophets.

_____
Date

Week 10 — Day 1 — Today's verses

1 Cor. 14:3 — But he who prophesies speaks building up and encouragement and consolation to men.

39 — So then, my brothers, desire earnestly the prophesying…

3:12 — But if anyone builds upon the foundation gold, silver, precious stones, wood, grass, stubble.

_____
Date

Week 10 — Day 2 — Today's verses

1 Cor. 14:12 — So also you, since you are zealous of spirits, seek that you may excel for the building up of the church.

24-25 — But if all prophesy and some unbeliever or unlearned person enters, he is convicted by all; the secrets of his heart become manifest; and so falling on *his* face, he will worship God, declaring that indeed God is among you.

_____
Date

Week 10 — Day 3 — Today's verses

1 Cor. 14:31 — For you can all prophesy one by one that all may learn and all may be encouraged.

Rom. 1:14-15 — I am debtor both to Greeks and to barbarians, both to wise and to foolish; so, for my part, I am ready to announce the gospel to you also who are in Rome.

_____
Date

Week 11 — Day 4

Today's verses

Exo. 30:23-25   You also take the finest spices: of flowing myrrh five hundred *shekels*, and of fragrant cinnamon half as much, two hundred fifty *shekels*, and of fragrant calamus two hundred fifty *shekels*, and of cassia five hundred *shekels*, according to the shekel of the sanctuary, and a hin of olive oil. And you shall make it a holy anointing oil, a perfume compounded according to the perfumer's art; it shall be a holy anointing oil.

1 John 2:20   And you have an anointing from the Holy One, and all of you know.

Date _____

Week 11 — Day 5

Today's verses

2 Cor. 4:10   Always bearing about in the body the putting to death of Jesus that the life of Jesus also may be manifested in our body.

16   Therefore we do not lose heart; but though our outer man is decaying, yet our inner *man* is being renewed day by day.

Rom. 8:13   For if you live according to the flesh, you must die, but if by the Spirit you put to death the practices of the body, you will live.

Gal. 5:24   But they who are of Christ Jesus have crucified the flesh with its passions and its lusts.

Date _____

Week 11 — Day 6

Today's verses

1 John 5:6   This is He who came through water and blood, Jesus Christ; not in the water only, but in the water and in the blood; and the Spirit is He who testifies, because the Spirit is the reality.

1 Cor. 15:10   But by the grace of God I am what I am; and His grace unto me did not turn out to be in vain, but, on the contrary, I labored more abundantly than all of them, yet not I but the grace of God which is with me.

45   …The last Adam *became* a life-giving Spirit.

Gal. 2:20   I am crucified with Christ; and *it is* no longer I *who* live, but *it is* Christ *who* lives in me…

Date _____

Week 11 — Day 1

Today's verses

Acts 13:33   That God has fully fulfilled this *promise* to us their children in raising up Jesus, as it is also written in the second Psalm, "You are My Son; this day have I begotten You."

1 Pet. 1:3   Blessed be the God and Father of our Lord Jesus Christ, who according to His great mercy has regenerated us unto a living hope through the resurrection of Jesus Christ from the dead.

1 Cor. 15:45   …The last Adam *became* a life-giving Spirit.

Date _____

Week 11 — Day 2

Today's verses

Matt. 22:32   "I am the God of Abraham and the God of Isaac and the God of Jacob"? He is not the God of the dead, but of the living.

Heb. 7:25   Hence also He is able to save to the uttermost those who come forward to God through Him, since He lives always to intercede for them.

Rom. 4:25   Who was delivered for our offenses and was raised for our justification.

John 12:24   Truly, truly, I say to you, Unless the grain of wheat falls into the ground and dies, it abides alone; but if it dies, it bears much fruit.

Date _____

Week 11 — Day 3

Today's verses

John 7:37-39   Now on the last day, the great day of the feast, Jesus stood and cried out, saying, If anyone thirsts, let him come to Me and drink. He who believes into Me, as the Scripture said, out of his innermost being shall flow rivers of living water. But this He said concerning the Spirit, whom those who believed into Him were about to receive; for the Spirit was not yet, because Jesus had not yet been glorified.

1 Cor. 15:45   …The last Adam *became* a life-giving Spirit.

Date _____

Week 12 — Day 1   Today's verses

1 John 2:15   Do not love the world nor the things in the world. If anyone loves the world, love for the Father is not in him.

5:19   We know that we are of God, and the whole world lies in the evil one.

1 Tim. 6:17   Charge those who are rich in the present age not to be high-minded, nor to set their hope on the uncertainty of riches but on God, who affords us all things richly for our enjoyment.

Date _____

Week 12 — Day 2   Today's verses

Luke 16:9   And I say to you, Make friends for yourselves by means of the mammon of unrighteousness, so that when it fails, they may receive you into the eternal tabernacles.

13   No household servant can serve two masters; for either he will hate the one and love the other, or he will hold to one and despise the other. You cannot serve God and mammon.

Date _____

Week 12 — Day 3   Today's verses

1 Cor. 16:1-3   Now concerning the collection for the saints, just as I directed the churches of Galatia, so you also do. On the first day of the week each one of you should lay aside in store to himself whatever he may have been prospered, that no collections be made when I come. And when I arrive, whomever you approve, I will send them with letters to carry your gift to Jerusalem.

Acts 4:32   And the heart and soul of the multitude of those who had believed was one; and not even one said that any of his possessions was his own, but all things were common to them.

Date _____

Week 12 — Day 4   Today's verses

1 Cor. 16:2-3   On the first day of the week each one of you should lay aside in store to himself whatever he may have been prospered, that no collections be made when I come. And when I arrive, whomever you approve, I will send them with letters to carry your gift to Jerusalem.

Matt. 6:3-4   But you, when you give alms, do not let your left hand know what your right hand is doing, so that your alms may be in secret; and your Father who sees in secret will repay you.

Date _____

Week 12 — Day 5   Today's verses

Luke 16:9   And I say to you, Make friends for yourselves by means of the mammon of unrighteousness, so that when it fails, they may receive you into the eternal tabernacles.

6:38   Give, and it will be given to you; a good measure, pressed down, shaken together, and running over, they will give into your bosom. For with what measure you measure, it shall be measured to you in return.

Acts 20:35   ...It is more blessed to give than to receive.

Date _____

Week 12 — Day 6   Today's verses

Phil. 4:10   But I rejoiced in the Lord greatly because now at length you have caused your thinking for me to blossom anew; for which matter you had indeed taken thought, but lacked opportunity.

15   And you yourselves also know, Philippians, that in the beginning of the gospel, when I went out from Macedonia, no church had fellowship with me in the account of giving and receiving except you only.

19   And my God will fill your every need according to His riches, in glory, in Christ Jesus.

Date _____